What People are Saying About Dawn Callan and *Awakening the Warrior Within*:

". . . awakens the warrior spirit within each of us and points the way to true security and self-confidence, beyond the constraints of our own fears . . . an important and moving book."
Shakti Gawain
bestselling author

". . . gives a very important message to women—a message of power and enablement so that we don't have to walk around constantly in a state of fear."
Sonya Friedman,
television host, *Sonya Live* – CNN

"Written with honesty, wisdom, and clarity, this book offers hope to those seeking a deeper form of safety and freedom."
Christina Grof,
author of *Thirst for Wholeness*

"Teaches us how to stand up for ourselves and our planet . . . challenges us to awaken to our own authentic strength and purpose."
Nan Stockholm,
environmental attorney, former counsel
U.S. Senate Environmental Committee and
Chief of Staff U.S. Senator Bill Bradley

"Dawn taught me how to find in myself whatever I need to take care of myself."
Dianne Ross,
winner of "Tough Target Award," CBS TV, Chicago

"This work will take you to the brink of your greatest fear and draw you through it to a side of tremendous empowerment."
Dr. Linda Peterson, Ph.D.
University of Nevada Medical School

"I am the author of five published books and one video on the subject of street self-defense. As an instructor of survival myself, I see your course as a solution to a serious systems glitch. I have never before seen the 'warrior' awakened so effectively without massive trauma."
Marc MacYoung
Glendale, CA

"The course was the most helpful life-changing experience I have had in such a short amount of time. I will not ever have to be a victim in any circumstances: on the street, at home, at work, or in relationship."
Judy Bayens M.A.
Community Counseling & Personal Growth Ministry
Grand Rapids, MI

"I have owned my own business since 1983. After the workshop I broke the elusive six-figure barrier I had not been able to reach. . . ."
Lyn Pfaelzer
Pfaelzer Communications, CA

"At the interview (for a new job) I was able to draw upon the knowledge and insights from the workshop. I'm now Director of P.R. and Advertising for RE/MAX of Michigan. My employer said one of the key factors in hiring me was that he sensed I would not be afraid to stand up to him when it was necessary . . . nor let anyone else back me into a corner."
Jackie Olsen
Plainweed, MI

"To know what I can do because I have done it is (oddly) calming. I don't feel more powerful as much as I feel more at ease. I know it has to do with letting go of fear."
Janet Bridgers
Bridgers Public Relations
West Hollywood, CA

Awakening the Warrior Within

AWAKENING THE WARRIOR WITHIN

Secrets of Personal Safety and Inner Security

Dawn Callan

TENACITY PRESS

AWAKENING THE WARRIOR WITHIN
Secrets of Personal Safety and Inner Security

© 1995, 1999, Dawn Callan

Published by Tenacity Press
P.O. Box 2710
Ukiah, CA 95482
1-800-738-6721

Cover art and design by Greg Wittrock
Cover redesign by ChromaGraphics
Typography by TBH Typecast, Inc.

The author of this book does not dispense medical advice nor prescribe the use of any technique as a form of treatment for physical or mental problems without the advice of a physician either directly or indirectly. In the event you use any of the information in this book, neither the author nor the publisher can assume any responsibility for your actions. The intent of the author is only to offer information of a general nature to help you in your quest for personal growth.

Library of Congress Cataloging-in-Publication Data available.

Callan, Dawn, 1943–
    Awakening the warrior within : secrets of personal safety and inner security / Dawn Callan.
        p.   cm.
    ISBN 0-9656056-9-8 (trade pbk. : alk. paper)
    1. Self-actualization (Psychology)   2. Security (Psychology)
    3. Peace of mind.   4. Spiritual life.   I. Title.
    BF637.S4C34   1999
    158'.1—dc20   98-061698
                                                              CIP

First printing, March 1995
Second printing 1999
Printed in the U.S.A.

10   9   8   7   6   5   4   3   2

To Robert
and to Patrick, who got me through

Preface

*M*ANY OF US feel deeply concerned about the way violence continues to escalate in our society—in our entertainment media, on our streets and even in our families. More and more people feel unsafe in their neighborhoods and even in their own homes. And because we have done so much violence to our environment, we are even feeling that our planet is no longer safe.

While our leaders cast about for solutions, our individual efforts to change what is happening leave us increasingly frustrated and fearful. However, Dawn Callan's work opens our eyes to a very different set of perspectives—the spiritual, psychological, and physical roots of the problem. And here we discover the source of the personal sense of disempowerment that so many of us are experiencing. What's more, she offers options that each of us can choose right now. Drawing from her many years of training and experience in spiritual and physical disciplines, Dawn teaches us how to reconnect with the natural power of the warrior within each of us, and how to use that energy to reclaim a sense of confidence and safety in our lives.

There is much confusion, individually and culturally, about the proper role of this warrior energy. As we evolve in consciousness, it is clear that we can no longer use it for warfare and killing. We seek, instead, a life-affirming expression of this energy. Looking further, we find that within the heart of the warrior is the pure essence of the life force itself. Without that force we lose the power to take care of ourselves, to feel strong and secure, to stand up for what we believe, and to fight for Mother Earth.

In this book, the author shares with us her best understanding of the *evolved warrior,* in its purest expression of the life force, embracing all life the world over. She shows us, in practical ways, how we can develop and express this warrior energy so that we may all enjoy inner and outer peace.

I believe that everyone who reads this book will benefit from Dawn Callan's important insights, just as I have.

Shakti Gawain

Acknowledgments

*M*Y thanks to Hal Zina Bennett, my mentor and muse, disguised as an editor. His sense of humor kept everything in perspective. His confidence in me taught me to find the *writer within*. Never afraid to share his own brillance, he teaches others to find their own light.

To Susan J Sparrow, who kept it all together in the fourth dimension, against all odds (many of which we provided). She kept us grounded, and made it happen.

To the rest of the Warrior team: Mari, sister, sorcerer's apprentice and friend, and Christopher and Joel, without whom it wouldn't be possible or, more to the point, nearly as much fun.

And to Tracy, newly among us. Hang on to your hat!

Table of Contents

What This Book Is About

*T*HIS BOOK IS ABOUT the journey back to power. It is a path we are all on whether we know it or not. In my own life this path has often seemed to wander. But looking back, I can see that I was guided every step of the way. To whatever degree my understanding allowed me to follow that guidance, the journey was easy. To whatever degree I resisted, the journey was difficult until I learned to trust the guidance and to honor the resistance as my teacher.

The journey of a warrior is always a journey back to ourselves. There are many challenges and obstacles along the way and most of them have to do with fear. Fear, like resistance, is always a great teacher and as we progress we learn to treat both of these as allies rather than adversaries. Our toughest opponents are often our greatest teachers. We learn about the edge between freedom and fear and how the warrior rides that edge.

Now more than at any other time in recorded history is the time for the warrior in each of us to act:

To stand up to tyranny,
To stand up to violence,

To act with integrity,
To act with commitment,
To act with compassion.

Each act of power transforms fear to freedom.
Each act of courage loosens the bond of tyranny.
Each act of integrity brings the truth into clearer
    focus.
Each act of compassion opens our hearts to love.

The warrior's path is not without risk. It means leaving the relative safety of the known, no longer locked in our homes against intruders, no longer locked in our safe perception of reality. It means opening ourselves up to other possible truths and stepping into the unknown.

A warrior understands that there is an inner web, a connectedness with all things. He or she knows the difference between autonomy and separation. Autonomy is the understanding that as each of us acts in our own truth, that action blesses everyone.

Separation is the belief that what I do over here, doesn't impact you over there, so I can act as if I live in a vacuum, with no consequence or benefit to anyone else.

A warrior knows that actions and thoughts have consequences, and that there are no isolated acts.

At the beginning of our workshops on the Warrior Within we often have students tell us how they resent living in a world with so much fear and violence. As the participants express their deepest feelings, one central fact becomes clear: this is the world we have created. These are the rules we have laid down. And now we must play by them.

If we are to live in peace with one another, and in harmony with the rest of the planet, there is much we have to do. The first step is to connect with the part of ourselves that is up to the task. That part is our warrior.

If we are going to survive as a species, we are going to have to change the way we relate to ourselves, each other, and the planet. It will take a lot of courage, perseverance, compassion, honesty, and wisdom to do so. These are the qualities of an evolved warrior. We take our warrior into our personal work to give us the honesty to face ourselves. We take our warrior's heart, and the warrior's willingness to risk everything into our relationships, so that we can learn to trust and be trusted. We take our warrior's will out into the world, to face the tyrants that would destroy it, and we work to restore balance and harmony. But the experience of our warrior in each moment of our daily lives, in our everyday reality, is just as significant as the larger tasks at hand. We call on our inner warrior when we say a difficult truth to a loved one, set a boundary with a co-worker and stand up for it, risk an adventure, rescue an animal, ask for a raise, start our own business, reach out to someone who's afraid to ask for help, or when we ask for help when we need it. It is feeling alive, feeling connected, feeling afraid and doing something anyway, experiencing our lives as our adventure, and living our lives as our art.

An important aspect of warrior work is what we are teaching our children. They are our future. Recently on the news there was a story about a young girl who was abducted by a stranger. Fortunately, she was found alive the next day. Unfortunately, it seems she went with her abductor without a struggle.

Polly Klaas walked out of her home with her abductor, in front of two other young girls, with her mother asleep in the next room. She also went without a struggle. Unfortunately, she was not found alive. Had those three girls known how, they could have rat-packed the man and taken him down.

I guess my question is, what are we teaching our children that they are not resisting violence? What must they think of themselves if they compliantly go off with strangers to get raped and murdered? Most of us want our children to relate to the world as a loving and friendly place—and most of the time it is. So it can be difficult to imagine that there might be a way to have our kids grow up not only with a positive outlook on the world but also with the skills to recognize real danger when it is present and defend themselves when it is necessary. Up to now, most parents have not had available to them a way to accomplish this.

Our culture has been so invested in suppressing the warrior that it has sacrificed its women and children. Not only are we not taught how to protect ourselves, but taught instead that we are not even able, that we must depend on men for our defense.

One of the things we need to do, and are beginning to do, as warriors, and as parents, is to no longer stand by and watch it happen. If we began teaching self-defense to our kids—boys and girls—starting in grade school, we'd eliminate a lot of the problem. We've got room for home-ec in the curriculum; I'd rather see little girls learn to kick than cook. We need to let our little girls claw and growl when threatened. When we banish the wild child, we begin to banish the warrior, and we leave our children defenseless.

There are a lot of predators out there right now. By definition of the word they are preying on the weak and helpless. It's a sad statement about this culture, but "little" and "helpless" is a turn-on for a lot of people in this country. Child abuse is rampant, and one out of every three women in this country will be raped in her lifetime. Women and children have been deprived of warriorship in this country. Part of warrior work is getting clear as a society about what we have to do so that women and children won't be victims anymore. When women take their power back and learn how to take care of themselves, and when we teach our children how to identify danger, and protect themselves from violence, the predators will be encouraged to heal their own wounds so that they no longer need to act out their pain.

The best thing we can do to protect our kids is teach them how to protect themselves. Teach them how to identify danger, to trust their instincts, teach them that they don't have to be nice to someone they don't trust, that they can snarl at strangers and draw their boundaries with people they know.

Our children should be our treasures. One of the measures of the values of a culture is in how it values its children.

Remember how scary it was not having mentors, or heroes, and having to find them in comic books or on TV?

As we awaken our own inner warriors, and become better models, and take the time to be mentors, we'll find a way to create a world where the little warriors coming through never get put to sleep.

What we have suffered from is fear of mastery. As masters we have to be individual, unique, and accountable. We have to come out and be separate. We are being asked to leave our parents' house, where we know that if we abide by their rules, we'll be taken care of. As long as we stay there, we don't get to express who we really are, because we might get sent to our room without dinner. But at least we get dinner. We may need to be a little hungry to be happy. No more excuses, no more slack. No more equivocating.

We have the ability to recognize the areas of our life where our victim operates, to understand how we were wounded, and recognize how our energy works. We have the ability to learn what it takes to set our boundaries. We have the ability to learn how to stand up to our tyrants. We have all the tools necessary to make our lives work, and we are remembering that we've always had the tools.

In this book we explore not only what it means to be a warrior, but also the qualities that we might develop if we wish to become warriors ourselves. It is my fondest hope that in this exploration of the spirit of the warrior you might discover these same qualities in yourself and carry them forward in your daily life, helping to make this world not only safer on a physical level, but nurturing to the spirit as well.

As we awaken the warrior within us, we begin to see the challenges of our lives in a different light. Rather than feeling victimized, we begin to feel that overcoming these challenges actually carries us to new levels of mastery. The stories our students tell us about the victories they experience as the result of their reclaiming their inner warrior never cease to inspire us and reaffirm our belief in this work.

While we do hear many stories about physical confrontations, in which our students are able to prevent or fight off their would-be aggressors, some of the most satisfying feedback comes from people who achieve mental and emotional victories through this work. These stories are always exciting to hear because they tell us how valuable these skills are for meeting the challenges of everyday life, and for building a positive sense of oneself. Of particular importance are those reports where the experiences of the workshop help people toward a very deep healing of previous wounds which had been limiting their lives and having a negative affect on their self-esteem. I particularly recall the story of a young woman I'll call Sally.

Several years before taking the workshop, Sally had been abducted and raped. The experience destroyed her self-confidence and self-esteem. During the workshop, she learned specific tools and techniques for handling the situation should it ever happen again. With her permission we reenacted portions of the incident, giving her the opportunity to use her new tools to reclaim her power in the present. During the reenactment, she accessed her warrior and successfully defended herself in a way she'd never done before. This helped her heal the inner wounds she had suffered as a result of her abduction. But on a more immediate matter, it gave her new courage to face a bitter divorce and custody suit scheduled for court the following week.

Sally's estranged husband claimed that she had been so debilitated by her abduction that she was now incapable of taking care of her children. This was his argument for getting custody of their children. Prior to the workshop, Sally's biggest fear was that she would cave in during the court hearing if anyone brought up the subject of the abduction—and she had no doubt her ex-husband would do exactly that. Because she had reexperienced the abduction and gotten in touch with her personal power around it, she now felt strong and in charge of her own life. And she knew how to fight.

When the hearing was over she called and told us that she'd won her battle. She would retain custody of her children. What's more, the judge had been so offended by the way her ex-husband talked about Sally during the hearing that he leaned down from the bench and told him: "If I ever see you in my court again you had better bring your toothbrush because you are going to jail!"

In a similar but less dramatic vein, I like to share Frank's story of the personal victory he experienced following his attendence in one of our workshops. As a child, he had been sexually abused and had spent his entire adult life living with guilt and shame. He was so shamed by his experience that he had withheld this information from both his therapist and his wife, and most of the time he hid it from himself. During the workshop, he found the courage to share his *dark secret* with his wife. His fear had always been that if she found out about it she would no longer love him. The day he told her, he discovered just the opposite was true: She loved him even more for the courage and honesty it required for him to reveal his hidden and shamed self to her. The result in their marriage was that they both got to share greater intimacy and trust. On an individual basis, Frank freed himself of a huge emotional burden and came to enjoy greater self-acceptance and self-love.

There is so much to be learned about ourselves and each other, and the more we do learn the more we discover how much of the human experience we all share and have in common. Regardless of which gender we are, what economic or social backgrounds we come from, or what nationality or race we are, we are much more alike than we are different. This becomes increasingly clear as we awaken the warrior within.

We have an enormous task ahead of us, to reclaim our power and our wholeness, and to break our addiction to violence and tyranny and fear.

The message the warrior has to deliver is that we have everything we need to accomplish that task.

The Ten Universal Laws
of the Warrior Code

*T*HROUGHOUT THIS BOOK you'll find references to the Ten Universal Laws of the Warrior Code, and how our lives can be enriched through observing them. Here is a complete list of these laws, which you'll also be discovering in the following pages.

1. *Pay Attention.*
   Stay in the present. It's the only place anything is really happening.
2. *Take Responsibility.*
   This is your life, take it back. Either you get to own it, or you blame someone or something else for it. Choose.
3. *No Kvetching.*
   No whining, no sniveling—it takes you out of the present and lets you abdicate responsibility.
4. *Don't Take Any Shit.*
   It's very bad for one's self-esteem to take any abuse. Stand up to your tyrants, both internal and external. The cost is too great not to.
5. *Do It Anyway.*
   Hard choices temper our strength and our integrity; they make the difference between a life of mediocrity and a life of excellence.
6. *Don't Quit.*
   Look at what stops you, at where you give the effort up. That is the edge between becoming a victim or a warrior.

7. *Keep Your Agreements.*
   A warrior is only as good as his or her word. The way
   we build self-trust and trust in others is by making
   and keeping our agreements.

8. *Keep Your Sense of Humor.*
   Otherwise what's the point? Humor helps us to
   stretch beyond ourselves and our own limits.

9. *Love One Another.*
   Otherwise where's the meaning? It's the way we
   remember we're not alone in this universe.

10. *Honor Your Connection to Source.*
    There is a force in the universe, greater than our-
    selves, that creates us, sustains us, provides for us,
    cares for us, guides us, and loves us. It speaks to us
    from within. Trust it.

My Story

J SOMETIMES THINK that my own warrior's journey began even before the womb. Born to alcoholic parents, my brother and sister and I came into a world that was totally unpredictable, often physically dangerous, and certainly very confusing. Among the things that saved me were the spontaneous moments of grace. I had my first experience of epiphany when I was about five years old. I was sitting in my backyard when I had the sense of everything in my world shifting. Everything I had thought to be separate from me I experienced as a part of me. I understood that everything I had thought to be real was an illusion. I felt as if I were waking from a dream. I remember looking at this new landscape and thinking, "Who am I, really?" I knew in that moment that my life was going to be extraordinary. Although the experience did not recur for many years, that moment became a touchstone for me, a place I could trust in the midst of pain and confusion, a point more real than the day-to-day physical reality. It was a place I could return to in memory when I had no place else to turn.

Because of my mother's radical mood swings and wildly erratic behavior, fueled by her drinking, we were constantly subjected to both physical and emotional attacks. If only because I was the oldest child in our family, it became my duty early on to keep my brother and sister and me safe. This included standing between them and mother when she went into a violent rage. I also vowed, early on, to one day take my brother and sister out of there, to someplace that we'd all be safe. I consider this the beginning of my warrior training. It wasn't until many years later that I was able to recognize this. I felt as if I had been drafted and had not volunteered. I know now this wasn't so.

I remember my mother holding my infant sister at the top of the stairs one day in my grandparents' house. I was eight years old. It was early afternoon and mother was already quite drunk. She lost her balance and fell with my sister in her arms. I can see it as clearly today as the moment it happened, how my mother provided no protection for my sister as she fell. The instinct to surround her child with her own body as they fell simply wasn't there. When they hit the bottom I ran to them. There was quite a lot of blood and my mother was unconscious. I picked up my sister who miraculously wasn't hurt, but she was shrieking, something she did quite well throughout her entire childhood. I ran to get my great-grandmother to help my mother. She looked at my mother, assessed this as an opportunity to clean up the gene pool, herded me away from where my mother lay and said we should leave her there and take care of my sister. I know she was hoping my mother would die. My great-grandmother hated the way my mother treated us. I ran to the neighbor's for help and by the time I returned, my mother had resumed consciousness, such as it was. She was relatively unhurt. The alcohol had broken her fall. I can only assume the angels had broken my sister's.

I can't ever remember not fighting. In grade school, I'd make appointments for after-school fights with the toughest boys I could find. I'd come home bloody but victorious. Although I've always been small, I learned the value of intent very early on. If my will was stronger than my opponent's will, I would win. Most people quit right before they win.

My parents divorced when I was nine. This event was marked by our being awakened in the middle of the night and transported by train to our family's ranch in Virginia. Daddy didn't come; the reason was left to us to figure out.

From Virginia we moved to Naples, Florida, where my mother's parents had a home. Thereafter, my mother systematically went about her own destruction and the attempted destruction of her children. We never saw our father again. As time went on, my mother began to isolate herself, and us, from the rest of the family. She wanted no witnesses. We felt like hostages. Her brother, our Uncle George, and his wife Mary, provided the only intervention we knew. He did his best to be a father to us, to provide us with some sense of family, and normalcy. Uncle George was a man of courage and principle. He always kept his agreements. He became my model for these qualities as Aunt Mary became my first model of a feminist, long before the term was invented. She was independent and full of life, in contrast to our mother, who was full of death.

Our mother was a master of the blindside shot. Just when I thought I had all our defenses shored up, she'd slip one in and catch us unawares. For example, sitting down to Thanksgiving dinner one year, everything seemed to be going smoothly. It appeared that we were going to enjoy a calm and peaceful holiday. Then, without warning, and with no obvious provocation, mother flew into a rage, screaming epithets at everyone in her life. The episode came to a climax when she grabbed the turkey and hurled it across the room. I often wonder who she would have been had she turned all that energy to some good use. I realize she was my first sensei.* I learned to take a shot and recover, get knocked down and get back up.

---

* In the martial arts the *sensei* is the teacher, or master, providing opportunities for the student to discover his or her personal power.

When I was about sixteen, on a day in early spring in Naples, I remember taking off my shoes and putting my bare feet on the ground. I felt my feet connect with the ground, and the warmth of the earth shoot through my body like an electric current, and once again I was reminded of the Oneness, and I felt my connection to all things. I knew that in the midst of chaos was perfection. I remembered that I was not alone. I somehow knew I was going to be all right.

In junior high school, I began to study dance. By high school, I was teaching and had formed my own dance troupe, choreographing and performing locally. Dance was where I owned my strength and stamina and grace.

I left for college to continue to study dance, even though I was reluctant to leave my siblings in my mother's care. I knew I had to get on with my life, and make a place for them away from her.

I married in my freshman year and gave birth to my daughter, Kimberly. My desire for a child was great; at the time I saw it as a safe place to love. Through her I did indeed learn about unconditional love. I learned that love is never safe, but worth the risk.

I divorced Kimberly's father when she was two. In retrospect I saw that I had been looking for a sperm donor, not a commitment.

When I was 21 I received the news that my mother had cancer. I dropped out of college to care for her for the last few months of her life. I arrived at her home to find my brother and sister terrorized. They were still in their early teens at this time. Having accomplished her own destruction, she was hard about taking them down with her. I loved her, but hated what she was doing. I knew her death was the only way out for them.

I watched her take her last breath. She went out in a fury; she couldn't believe that something was out of her control. She clenched her jaw until it dislocated, grasped my hand with such force at the moment of her death, that I had to peel her fingers away after she was gone. I was terrified, but I knew we were free.

I kept my promise to my brother and sister to take them with me, even though my mother left them to someone else and I had to fight for their custody. She left them in her will to an alcoholic friend of hers, to complete what she had begun, albeit without the same skill. It was to be her parting shot to me, to render me helpless to save what I loved.

The level of my warrior skills was pretty rudimentary at that time, and I simply showed up at her friend's door and said, "I'm taking the kids with me, and if you try to stop me, I'll kill you." It lacked subtlety, but it worked. Basically, I was scared all the time, but I had a job to do and I did it anyway. Warrior Skills 101. If I hadn't been responsible for three other beings, I might have been tempted to give up. But I'd fought for them and now I had to stick around to care for them. Warrior Skills 201. It may have appeared that I saved them, but in the long run, they saved me.

We began a journey that led us through the changes of the sixties. All of the old social systems were breaking down and we were free to choose a new way of being. We let our hair grow; experimented with psychedelics; lived communally in Cambridge, Massachusetts, and Coconut Grove, Florida; questioned reality and studied metaphysics. We read the *Tao Te Ching, The Tibetan Book of the Dead,* and *Be Here Now.* We practiced yoga, became vegetarians, and stepped out of the main stream, never to reenter again. We stepped into a different flow. I dragged my brother, my sister, and my daughter, from saint, to sage, to guru. Hot after it. Looking for answers.

Even though we didn't know it, this was further warrior training in coming out and being separate, living our own truth even when it flew in the face of convention. We felt we were breaking new ground, clearing a path through the mine field. We stepped into the unknown, because what we had experienced so far wasn't working. We had to find another way. It's clear to me in retrospect (hindsight is always 20/20), that the Universe had put us into warrior boot camp.

I'll never forget my grandmother's funeral. My grandmother, Mommylou—my mother's mother—was very dear to me. She was one of my original models for wild women. My brother and sister and I showed up for the ceremony in various stages of drag. I was a full-blown hippie, with hair down to my butt and dilated pupils, wearing a variation of sackcloth and ashes. We were all serious students of yoga. I Insisted on kneeling in front of the coffin and reciting my mala, a Hindu version of the rosary, which caused the Catholic contingent in our family to turn their heads away and go into comfortable denial. My brother and sister were much more parochial in their attire and behavior, although they didn't fool me for a minute.

We had brought with us our friend Fred, replete with dreadlocks. Uncle George and Aunt Mary generously, if foolishly, offered to have all of us stay at their home. I refused, since I had to get up at 4 A.M. and chant, and didn't want to disturb them. My brother, Paul (or Pablo, or Vasu Dev, depending on your time frame) and Fred (or Maha Dev), accepted their offer. My Uncle George still tells the story of how he got up the next morning to find Fred out in the middle of his lawn, standing on his head.

Once again, in Cambridge, I was sitting alone when I was transported out of my normal reality and into a place where I experienced the perfection and Oneness of all being. Perhaps I should add that this happened spontaneously and without the use of any drugs. I felt as though I was held in God's embrace, and I knew that everything in the Universe was just as it should be, including what I considered suffering. I saw the perfection of the Divine plan. I knew that peace and bliss were everyone's heritage, and that eventually, everyone got home. I felt incredible love from and for everything. I knew that this was an experience of God, but also, I knew it to be an experience of who I really am. When I came out of this state, I recognized that this was the goal. I just needed to figure out the path. I eventually came to realize that it was the warrior's path that would consistently take me home, and that it was a path that I had been on all along, long before I was able to name it.

My brother and sister and I began to study yoga with a particular swami while we were in Coconut Grove. After several months I realized that the ashram politics resembled, on a subtler level, the way we were treated as children. I decided to get us out of there. I thanked the swami for his teaching and told him we needed to move on. He told me I was doomed. I packed the kids, the dogs, the cats, and the monkey into our Volkswagen camper and headed for Cambridge. It seemed as good a place as any to be doomed. My brother and sister soon left to return to the ashram. Fearful of the swami's influence, and afraid of losing my siblings, I followed them back to Coconut Grove. They were forbidden to see me. I was considered a bad influence, something I worked hard to live up to. I would ambush them outside the ashram and stayed in touch with them in spite of the swami. My sister left the swami several years ago, but my brother continues to be at the ashram. I continue to be a bad influence.

A Keseyesque bus trip took me to California for the first time in 1973. California felt like home. I felt physically nourished by its beauty, and I knew I had to live here. I packed my daughter, our dogs, and our few belongings, having unburdened ourselves of most material possessions along the way. Trading our Limoges for Melmac, we headed for Los Angeles.

A romance with a man I met there ended violently when I told him I needed to be on my own. In a rage, he threw me around like a rag doll. I had always felt like a fighter, but I was unable to react. I felt no fear or anger until later. A place in me simply observed. I felt paralyzed. I had lost the physical ability to fight I'd had as a child. I knew that something natural and instinctive had been conditioned out of me and I wanted it back. I picked myself up, grabbed my daughter and my dogs, and left in the middle of the night.

I realized an important message had been delivered. Although I had the spirit of a fighter, somewhere along the way I had lost my instinctual response to danger. This left me vulnerable. I knew I had to go after this missing piece if I was ever to feel safe. Because of the early experiences of my life, I didn't believe I could trust anyone else. This experience left me feeling that I couldn't trust myself.

I went looking for a martial arts teacher. I visited a number of schools and observed their classes until I watched a class in Choi Lai Fut. The movement spoke to me on a very deep level. I began studying with Frank Premecias, and felt as though I had found my path home. It was the beginning of a life's work.

I moved us to Northern California to follow a spiritual teacher, Hari Das Baba. Babaji was my first bodyguard job, a career I would resume years later. I traveled with him, took care of him, and set boundaries with his students. Babaji was himself a great warrior. The balance of power and compassion, fierceness, and kindness was an example I needed. I had kept my tender heart hidden inside a tough exterior all of my life, maintaining a constant state of hypervigilance, holding the line against danger. Babaji held the line with love. It was many years before I could embody that example and feel safe in my vulnerability.

I began studying Hop Gar Kung Fu in San Francisco with David Chin and simultaneously began training in Kenpo with Doug McLeod in Santa Cruz. I eventually earned a black belt from Doug. Doug gave me support and inspiration, believing in me when I doubted myself. One of the things I learned from Doug was the old axiom that has to do with leaving your teacher and learning to stand alone: "When you meet the Buddha in the road, kill him." Soon after earning my black belt from him, I broke contact with him. I needed to develop my own ideas and test them outside anyone else's system. My work is very nontraditional and I wanted space away from the approval or disapproval of my teachers. Doug kept track of me and my work and after many years, he came back into my life, when I had the confidence to meet him as an equal as well as honor him as a teacher.

He called to promote me to 5th degree black belt, which in our system is the level of Master. Not having followed the traditional methods for promotion, I was overwhelmed. He asked that I send him whatever I was working on, so I offered to send him a videotape done by Liz and Randy Love (Randy is an award-winning cinematographer). It is a documentary of my workshop that they produced on their own time and at their own expense, out of their respect for the work. I also offered to share the rough draft of this book. Doug said, "I will always ask your permission before I use anything of yours." I felt very acknowledged that my sensei could see me as his sensei, and felt everything come full circle. In that moment I got the final piece of the axiom, " If you meet the Buddha in the road, kill him." What the Buddha knows is that the Buddha doesn't die.

I also earned a black belt in Kobra Kaj Karate from Clinton Moscly. Clinton was one of the fiercest fighters I had ever seen. He brought to my art a level of reality and intention that I needed.

Doug has since promoted me to the level of 6th degree. Our friendship and respect for each other continues to grow.

Although I had great teachers, my martial arts career was often difficult. I had to face self-doubt, pain, humiliation, and time after time, my fear. There were many times I would pull off the road after a training and weep. There were times I wanted to quit, feeling it was just too hard. But I knew I couldn't quit, that this work was an essential part of what I had been brought into this world to do.

Right before my black belt test I began to hear a voice in my head. It said, "What do you need to take this test for? You've trained long and hard and you've already reached black belt level. What do you have to prove?" If I had listened to that voice I wouldn't be teaching warrior skills today. I would have closed a lot of doors instead of opening them. It was an important lesson for me in identifying the difference between fear that keeps one safe and the fear that holds one back.

I moved to Carmel Valley at my daughter's request that we quit moving while she was in high school. We had lived like gypsies and Kimberly had been my only constant, an anchor in my life. She had the wisdom to know what she needed and to ask for it. Using money from my inheritance, I bought a small ranch, a few Arabian horses, including a very lovely stallion, and began my career as a horse breeder with absolutely no clue as to what I was getting into. Arabians are full of fire and intelligence, and as teachers, they are uncompromising. Some of the best teachings about paying attention have come to me from horses. There are few things less forgiving than 1000 pounds of horse flesh if you lose your focus.

While living in the Valley, I began studying Christian Science. I had come from a Catholic background, studied Eastern religions, but had not found a healing system that was pragmatic and real to me. I had the privilege of studying with Paul Stark Seeley, and incorporated many of the principles he taught into my life.

Kimberly had a car accident when she was 16. I got the phone call every parent dreads, telling me she was in the emergency room. The medical prognosis was one of permanent disability and permanent disfigurement—a diagnosis we were not willing to accept. I picked her up off the table and took her home. We meditated and prayed for three days and at the end of that time, miraculously, she was completely healed. Although I no longer consider myself strictly a Scientist or Buddhist, or a Catholic for that matter, these faiths have all made a contribution to my life. I kept hearing the same message in all of them. We are always connected to Source. Everything we need is within us.

I opened a martial arts school, teaching both men and women. But I felt as though there was still a piece missing for me. That missing piece was delivered to me by the boyfriend of a potential student. A woman came to the school who wanted to study with me. She brought her skeptical boyfriend with her. He began testing me, grabbing and throwing punches. I responded in form, as I had been trained to do, pulling my technique back before it did any damage. He began to escalate his game since I was answering with theory and not with pain. He pushed harder, I continued to be nice, until I had my back to the wall in my own school. In that moment I felt my conscious mind recede and become only a witness. A surge of power shot up my spine. Everything became still, my senses opened up, everything became brighter, sharper, and seemed to be in slow motion. I felt as if my system had gone into overdrive. I knew that I had all the time and the resources I needed to take care of myself. I dropped him with a thrust kick to his jaw. After the job was done, the energy receded and my conscious mind stepped back in. I knew I had accessed a place in myself that had always been there but that had been put to sleep. Now it was wide awake.

The most significant quality of this state was that with the exception of my moments of epiphany, this was the first time in my life that I was totally without fear. However, unlike my epiphany states, I was not transported out of normal reality, but remained fully engaged and fully present. I knew that I would always have access to this place should I ever need it again. I knew that my life was changed forever. I knew that I would always be able to trust this part of myself. My martial arts and metaphysical training may have brought me to this place, but nothing had prepared me for the magnitude of the moment. I had met my inner warrior.

I began to design a system that would support others to reclaim their own inner warriors. I began to see how everything in my life had prepared me for this task. I knew that if for just one moment a person directly experienced who they really are, with all the filters removed and their inner critics silenced, their life would be changed forever. And as each individual remembers their true identity, the planet becomes a safer place.

This was the birth of the Warrior Within workshops. They have evolved over the years, with many people and many experiences contributing to their growth. I have come to understand that they deliver a message that needs to be heard at this time. The message is that we must face our fear. We must own it, take responsibility for it, and remember that its origin is within us.

We must remember that also within us is the warrior. This is the part of the self that stands up to fear, and in standing up to it, we will not be overwhelmed. We will be free.

Soon after the experience of meeting my inner warrior, everything in my life began to change. My daughter finished school and left home. My bucolic life as a horse rancher came to an end, and once again, I found myself on the brink of a new adventure. There was a part of me that never wanted to leave Carmel Valley, with its peace and pastoral beauty, but there were lessons to be learned elsewhere. I was developing my own self-defense system and I needed to test it outside the relative safety of a martial arts school.

I rented out my house, leased out my horses, and left for L.A. to start a security business, something I knew absolutely nothing about. Again, the teachers and teachings showed up for me and Aegis Protective Services was born. I stayed in L.A. for five years. Aegis gained a measure of success, and provided a great deal of excitement. We handled high-risk situations and high-profile clients. Short of joining the military or becoming a cop, this was as real as it gets. Aegis provided me with the opportunity to refine the physical self-defense system. I had access to expert martial artists and many of my operatives were ex-military or police. I trained with anyone who was willing to teach me, everything from hand-to-hand combat, firearms, and evasive driving. I was certified to teach police control and restraint techniques and use of the side-handle baton.

Simultaneously, I taught workshops in self-defense. I began to introduce more spiritual work into the physical system. Although it had always been endemic to my teaching, I began to see how tightly woven together are the inner and outer systems, and to understand what the great masters knew, that the martial arts is also a path to enlightenment.

As time went on, I introduced an additional element. I had always provided a teaching situation where teachers or other students would pretend to attack the students so they could experience how they might react if they were attacked in real life. But then I took this a step further. I decided to make the attacker an adversary that was bigger than life. I felt that if students could come up against what they believed to be impossible, and overcome it, it would change their belief in what was possible. That adversary showed up for me in the form of one of the agents working for Aegis. Robert Humphrey was, in every sense of the word, larger than life.

He was a formidable opponent, working the edge, not just physically but verbally and psychologically as well. He was the perfect tyrant. A highly skilled martial artist and stunt man, he was big, powerful, fast, intuitive, and ruthless (ruthlessness sometimes being the better part of compassion). He always managed to read where a student's worst fear was, and embody that fear. Students learned to access infinite, internal resources that are bigger than any external opponent. We saw breakthrough experiences, with students renegotiating old fears and traumas, finding their present point of power, and their lives were changed forever. Transformation became the standard of the work.

Robert contined to be a part of the work, actively as combat chief, as well as training our other attackers, until his untimely death on February 10, 1998. The qualifications for becoming a member of the combat team include a particular combination of skills: size, insight, skill level, heart, wisdom, intuition, compassion, dedication to a cause bigger than themselves, at considerable personal risk, and the ability to get their own ego out of the way and serve others with everything they are. There is no truer definition of a warrior. Robert, Patrick, and I looked for years for a backup combat team, and were unable to find anyone who fit the criteria until only months before Robert's death. The Universe always delivers, and we had found and were training Christopher Coppinger and Joel Morgan, two men who embody what it means to be a warrior. They have become integral to our team. We are grateful to have found them. Pat and I realized Robert wouldn't leave us until we had what we needed for the work. Robert's contribution to our work was enormous. We miss him every day.

While in L.A., I met my husband, Bob, a man so unlike the men I was usually attracted to that I didn't recognize him at first as my mate. I liked dangerous men. Bob expressed his power in a very different way. He was sensitive and intuitive with a highly developed feminine side. The first day we met, at a gym, we got into a four-hour, major, metaphysical conversation. We became best friends for a year before we fell in love. We shared everything: our lives, our dreams, we talked at least once a day on the phone, we cooked for each other (a skill he seems to have forgotten since we have been married), we talked about our romances with other people, gave each other advice, and developed a foundation of trust and friendship. I looked at him one day and knew I loved him. I realized that this was a man I could spend the rest of my life with. He may not have fit my mental pictures, but he fit my soul. Besides, I was dangerous enough for both of us.

We have been great teachers for each other, and mirrors for each other. It was from him that I learned how to trust another. It was from me that he learned about his warrior.

I decided to leave the security business and focus entirely on teaching the warrior workshops. Bob lost his job and was unable to find work and we decided it was time to leave L.A. We put everything in storage, rented a 22-foot RV, took our dog and cat and headed north, looking for home. We drove all the way up to Vancouver, B.C. and nothing spoke to us. On our way back down we drove into Marin County, California. I said to Bob, "Stop, this is it." Within a matter of days we found a house that we both loved and we relocated in San Anselmo.

The workshops grew through word of mouth. I taught only women until 1990. I had gotten many requests to develop a workshop for men by the men who saw the changes that took place in our graduates. I realized that warrior skills transcend gender, and created a workshop for men. The second workshop was given in Marin and was a pivotal workshop. Both Bob and our friend Pat Young participated in the workshop. At this point, Bob and I decided to teach together. Pat joined us as an attacker and now makes a brilliant contribution to the work. Pat is not only an excellent martial artist, he is also a student of metaphysics. One would swear that the members of our team are psychic (maybe they are) in their ability to reach inside of someone and pull out information. Pat knows how to bring a student face-to-face with their fear of the unknown, shows them where they abdicate responsibility as co-creators, where they don't trust themselves or the

Universe. He is a deeply spiritual man whose great faith has supported me through more than one difficult time.

We decided to make the workshops co-ed; the work became even more powerful, opening communication between men and women, breaking down the belief in polarity and allowing men and women to bear witness for each other as they reclaimed their power.

One of the things that makes our work unique is that it is designed to take participants to their edge, mentally, physically, spiritually, and psychologically, so that not only do they walk away knowing they can be responsible for their physical safety when they meet external tyrants, but that they can also face their internal tyrants. They get to see where they give their power away and how they can take it back. The opportunity for deep psychological work is profound.

As I have watched the workshop evolve, it is as if it has taken on a life of its own, drawing to it highly talented instructors and counselors, while attracting students who in their own right contribute so much, proving time and time again the resilience and potential expansiveness of the human soul. The growth of the workshop has been a reminder to me that life is about learning to trust ourselves and our own processes, and that when we do this the universe provides us with exactly what we need.

Today the workshops are tremendously powerful. They've become vehicles wherein people can discover their own inner sources of energy, self-esteem, strength, and joy. Sometimes, it is a matter of men and women recovering a sense of themselves that they had lost. At other times, it is a matter of them uncovering personal resources they had never even dreamed they had.

Betsy, for example, attended a workshop we gave at Sonoma State University, in northern California. She was confined to a wheelchair as the result of cerebral palsy but we quickly discovered that she had a great heart, spirit, and intelligence that more than made up for her physical limitations. Throughout the two-day workshop, she bravely explored and took charge of her greatest abilities. When her turn came for combat, she did well in the first two rounds, but she had an amazing breakthrough in the third. Robert, our "attacker," dramatically increased his aggression, pushing her beyond the point she believed she could go. Suddenly, she hurdled herself from her chair and slammed into Robert, knocking him down. She landed back in her wheelchair and proceeded to run right over him and then flee. I'm sure the look of exaltation I saw on her face that day will remain in my memory forever. So will the look of absolute incredulity on Robert's face! And so will the sound of the entire group leaping to their feet and cheering.

As a teacher, there is nothing more gratifying than seeing one's students come alive, discovering and then fully embracing their own previously buried capacities, then moving forward into a brand new way of living, filled with sheer delight and confidence.

One of the phrases we repeatedly use in the workshops is, "What have you got?" This means identifying the possibilities, techniques, target areas, weapons, and opportunities that are available. It means, no matter what, don't quit, and eventually you will find the resource you need to take care of yourself.

Josie, who is physically challenged from juvenile rheumatoid arthritis, was tested on the street three years after taking the workshop. She has very limited use of her arms and legs, and is very small—though that tiny body contains a powerful spirit. One evening she was walking home when a man grabbed her, threw her over his shoulder, and ran into an alley with her. Josie recalls, "I could tell my intent was a lot stronger than his, and he was not expecting any resistance. As he was carrying me down this alley, I suddenly saw Dawn's face, and she was yelling at me, "What have you got?" I turned and saw his right hand by my face and instantly reached over and bit his finger as hard as I could. He screamed, put me down and ran away."

What moves me most in all these stories, whether they are about physical victories or personal breakthroughs of a mental or emotional kind, is not so much that one person has prevailed over another because of what they've learned, but something bigger than that. Long ago I began to recognize that beyond the immediate exaltation was a deeper experience, an epiphany, that always teaches some essential truths about who we truly are and why we are here.

It has been experiences such as those I've already described, and many others I'll be sharing with you, that have inspired me to write this book. And it is my sincere wish that by the time you have finished reading these pages those same truths will have become a part of your life, always there to inspire you and constantly refresh your desire to continue pursuing the very best in yourself.

With the help of students, my publisher, and friends, I believe that we have captured in these pages the essence of what others have gotten from our workshops. And it is my sincere wish that every reader will be enriched by the gift of their own warriorship.

CHAPTER ONE

The Gift of Warriorship

*F*ROM A STRICTLY PRACTICAL point of view, the warrior is that part of us which acts with courage, with commitment, with integrity and compassion. It is our warrior self that sets boundaries, creating a safe space for us to live our lives. It is our warrior who faces fear and backs us up when we are in danger. It is our warrior who stands behind us as we renegotiate old wounds and trauma so that we may free ourselves from a painful past. The warrior stands up to tyrants, both internal and external, individual and collective. A warrior is accountable, self-disciplined, willing to serve a cause bigger than ourselves, and willing to do whatever it takes to get the job done.

Although I am an advocate of everyone learning how to defend themselves, and take responsibility for their own personal safety, this is not a book about the martial arts. This book is about the exploration of the internal qualities that make up a warrior, without which an external system won't work anyway. We're exploring a certain frame of mind, an aspect of our being, and aim at recognizing our true self and more fully realizing our true potential. The warrior's path is a

1

process of self-exploration and self-discovery. Warrior work is about learning how to fearlessly be ourselves in the world, and by doing so we find that we serve that world.

There is a new paradigm emerging in our culture, a new way of defining the warrior. Up until now, the warrior has been identified in most people's minds with shadow qualities, that is, domination and control over others, often through intimidation and physical force. At best the warrior was thought of as a hero, someone capable of isolated acts of bravery, but usually limited in abilities in other areas. We have the warrior represented in popular culture as the Terminator, or Rambo. They may be able to withstand a nuclear blast, but they cave in when confronted with the emotional realities of a relationship. This warrior/hero operates exclusively in our external reality, usually avoiding the inner world associated with emotional or spiritual well-being. While it is important to honor the part of ourselves that is willing to fearlessly hold the line against violence or danger, there is a different role the warrior has come to play in the present that is even more powerful and relevant for today's challenges: the role of the *spiritual warrior.*

There have been very few popular heroes who have embodied the values of the spiritual warrior. Kwai Chang Cane, in the television series *Kung Fu,* is as close as we get to a spiritual warrior hero figure in popular culture. What does the warrior have to do with spirituality? The values embodied by the spiritual warrior comprise the next step in our evolution as a species. How do I know this? I've paid attention. I've seen it reflected through our students and the way their lives have changed when they claim this part of themselves. I've seen it in my own life as I've struggled with and have finally been able to take in the lessons from my many teachers over the years. On a planetary scale as well, we're beginning to see that if we are to survive as a global community we can do so not through physical force and war but only through cooperation and love, and through an awareness of how we might serve a power greater than ourselves.

Beginning at a deeply personal level, warrior work is about waking up and standing up to whatever part of ourselves presents itself as an obstacle to our truth. By contrast, the old-style warrior, the archetype of shadow qualities, expressed by Rambo or the Terminator, would identify an enemy, separate it out, and defeat it. A spiritual warrior *stalks*, confronts, and finally integrates all of the parts of himself that would separate him from his wholeness. For example, let's say you discover as a sexually abused child that you still harbor a fear of intimate contact. The spiritual warrior first establishes physical safety, so that the abused inner child trusts you to protect him or her, then backs you up as you go through the old grief and pain. When it is appropriate, the spiritual warrior gives you the courage to confront your perpetrators and move beyond your pain and limitation. Eventually the spiritual warrior can help you confront the challenge of sustaining an intimate relationship.

"Spiritual" is a word many people are as uncomfortable with as they are with the word "sex." Many of us have been supported to believe that the spiritual is something so intangible and mysterious that only those ordained as "high priests" or gurus can understand it and communicate it to us. In many religious systems the spiritual is taught as something beyond our reach, a state of being we'll perhaps discover after we are dead, something to be achieved in another life. However, in this book we approach spirit in a very different way. Here you'll find that spirit lives in the present and the spiritual warrior is fully present, fully engaged in the moment. *Now* is the point of power. *Now* is the appointed hour.

Many religious systems teach that the world is an illusion. That doesn't mean we get to ignore it and avoid taking responsibility for it until the real thing comes along. The illusions we live with each day are our creations and we need to learn how to handle them well. For example, we have individually and collectively created illusions that have made it possible for us to destroy our rain forests, pollute the air and water, and create social environments in our inner cities that are violent and filled with despair and hopelessness. This means that as spiritual warriors we must at this time focus on bringing ourselves back into alignment with ourselves, each other, and Grandmother Earth.

Consciousness creates, and as spiritual warriors we are responsible for what we create. In the same way that a Higher Power has created us and cares for us, we create our world and care for it. A spiritual warrior's task is to identify with what is universal and permanent: that is the goal. To deal with what is in the present is the spiritual warrior's path. Spiritual is anything that supports our direct connection to Source, to whatever Power created our Universe and has given us life. Our spirituality is the part of ourselves that is infinite and eternal, that which is immutable. It is our ability to love, to experience joy, to be passionate, to be open and awake; it is our sense of humor, the capacity to embrace our own gifts and be ourselves in the world, to find ourselves in the Silence, to feel our connection to All That Is and to not take ourselves too seriously. It is dedication to the Universal and Eternal, what was once described to me as, "That which applies to all equally."

As spiritual warriors we learn to experience ourselves as expressions of a Greater Intelligence: our warrior trusts that intelligence to guide and care for itself and in turn we trust our warrior to guide and care for us.

*F*ACING OUR FEAR

It is impossible to define our spirituality without defining fear. The warrior's greatest task at this time is to help us identify and stand up to our fear. Everything in the Universe has a purpose. Nothing was created to do us harm, but we have been given free will and are able to take ourselves out of alignment with Universal Will if we choose. When we make that choice to separate ourselves from Universal Will, we experience ourselves as alienated from Source, and from each other. We see ourselves as competing with all others around us, giving rise to anger, fear, and the belief that if we are to survive we must learn to dominate and control everything around us. We step out of the flow and into struggle. While the original and natural purpose for fear was a part of our internal warning system, our instincts, our autonomy (it was intended to keep us safe and in alignment with Universal Will), there are ways we can distort or misuse it.

There are two primary forces operating in the Universe: love and fear. We fear what we are separate from. We attempt to cast out the parts of ourselves we refuse to own. These parts galvanize and show up in our lives in any number of ways, and they tyrannize us until we are willing to own them When we disown the parts of ourselves we dislike or fear, we find them mirrored back to us in our world, in our work, in our relationships, in any way that they can get our attention until we are finally willing to embrace them as part of ourselves. The spiritual warrior is the part of us that has the courage, the strength, and the compassion to include all of what we are—what we love as well as what we fear—and to recognize in doing so that we ultimately are able to enjoy our wholeness. Your warrior knows that who you are is big enough for all of life.

> Fear separates: Love unites.
> Fear excludes: Love includes.
> Fear contracts: Love expands.
> Love can include fear but fear cannot include love.
> What we fear owns us.
> What we love frees us.

> Fear of lack keeps us in poverty.
> Fear of love keeps us alone.
> Fear of our divinity keeps us asleep.

Your warrior is here to give you the courage, the intention, the resources, the perseverance, the strategy, the ruthlessness, the tenacity, the integrity, the patience, the will, the commitment, and the compassion to embrace your fear and transform it. Through your warrior you are able to face your fear, own it, to learn that fear has the power to create, and to see what fear has created in your life. The spiritual warrior can guide us to take responsibility for our creations, and transform the darkness we bring into our lives, so that we may stand in the light of love.

How do we change? How do we move out of the world of separation and fear, with all its terror and discontent? The short answer is that we pay attention until we become conscious about how we ourselves are creating our experience of life. The longer answer is described in the remaining pages of this book.

$\mathcal{V}$IOLENCE, FEAR, AND THE WARRIOR'S LOVE

Everyone is afraid of violence, and with good reason. It is always aimed at destruction. Violence is rampant in our culture. Many of the things we have done as a society to protect ourselves from growing violence have unfortunately only compounded our fears. For example,

1. We have identified the enemy/problem as something that lives outside ourselves.
2. We have separated it further from ourselves by punishment or banishment.
3. We have pumped up our army of shadow warriors (cops and military), to deal with it.
4. We have separated ourselves from this army because it embodies the same qualities as the enemy, and uses the same tactics the enemy uses.
5. We continue to polarize all the way through our adversarial legal system, and our love/hate relationship with attorneys.
6. We have put as much distance as we can between ourselves and the external problem so that we don't have to deal with the fact that the problem originates within ourselves.

Our fear of poverty is virtually universal. But instead of confronting our fear and seeking workable solutions, we do everything we can to avoid being reminded of it. Since looking at people who are living in poverty is one of the things that stirs up our fear, we shove them into areas we don't have to visit—at least not very often. We shun the inner cities and remote rural areas where poverty is so prevalent, until it has to explode in our faces in order to be recognized at all. We are one of the most affluent nations on this planet, yet one out of every three of our children lives in poverty. And we wonder why we have gangs of armed children in our streets.

As a culture we are fascinated with violence. We raise our children on it. Nobody wants to believe that if a four-year-old watches ten murders and twenty violent acts a day, all of which are readily absorbed into the unconscious mind, that the child is going to learn to be violent. And yet, everything we've ever learned about the human psyche in its formative years tell us this is so.

We have let the tiger out of its cage and now we are desperately trying to get it back in, beat it back in, shoot it back, bludgeon it back, because we are afraid it will devour us. Which of course it will unless we remember that we ourselves are the tiger.

Each of us has our own private tiger as well as the collective ones. I had a dream many years ago that helped me in my process of reclaiming my personal tiger. I dreamt that a woman dressed in white and holding a lamp entered the mouth of a cave and began a deep descent into the underground. She walked fearlessly, with purpose, and finally came to the end of the tunnel where there was a heavy iron door with thick bars on it. She pulled on the handle and opened it effortlessly. It wasn't locked, so she entered. Sitting in the middle of this dark cell, was a huge, hideous, beast. It hunkered down on all fours, covered with scales and hair and was terrifying looking. Showing no fear whatsoever, she simply said to it, "Follow me," then turned and began her ascent. The beast lumbered after her, at first unable to even stand upright, but as they walked toward the surface, it began to change.

The scales fell away, the hair disappeared. It stood up and with each step became more human and more beautiful, until by the time they emerged from the mouth of the cave, he was a radiant, gorgeous man. When they were out of the cave, she turned to face him and said, "Kneel," which he did. She placed a hand on his head and said, "Now you serve the Lady."

I realized from this dream that there is no part of ourselves that wasn't meant in some way to serve us if we are willing to own it, acknowledge it, and allow it to fulfill its higher purpose.

The spiritual warrior knows that we cannot slay the beast, or cage the tiger without destroying some part of ourselves. Our warrior helps us to reclaim the parts of ourselves we have lost so that we once again have access to their gifts, which are our own gifts. When we are able to face the parts of ourselves that we fear, we no longer need to live with each other as enemies.

How do we know where to begin our work to reclaim the power and guidance of our warrior? We look for the resistance in ourselves; we look to see where we have identified other people or forces outside of ourselves as the enemy. We identify the areas in our lives where we have polarized or created adversarial situations. When we find the resistance we press into it. When we encounter an enemy we find a way to make them an ally. We find the separate poles within ourselves and balance them.

My father was a hero in World War II, but in reality I believe he was a coward. He eventually abandoned himself to alcohol and he abandoned his children. He didn't have the courage to face his own flaws or work out the day-to-day domestic difficulties necessary for making a family.

I have come to believe very firmly that the real acts of heroism, the actions of a true spiritual warrior are measured by the moment-to-moment acts of integrity and personal courage in our daily lives. A person may have the courage to rescue someone from a burning building, but not have the courage to rescue themselves from their own isolation. A person may be willing to risk the perils of war, but be unable to risk the perils of an intimate relationship. The spiritual warrior guides us through the dark places in our world, and in ourselves, lighting the way for our future and teaching us to live in our present. It is to those ends that this book is dedicated.

*Z*RY THIS

Take a moment and find for yourself one thing you have done today that expresses courage. It may have been revealing a difficult truth to someone, or making an unselfish choice about something that maybe no one else would ever know.

If you can't think of anything, the fact that you are reading this book means you have the courage to look for your own inner hero. Accepting this as your new path, find a way to make a contribution, no matter how small, to someone else, or some part of Grandmother Earth.

Those of us who are called to warrior work will have a great deal asked of us. It is not a path without risk; it is also not without rewards. As each of us is willing to live more impeccably, and demand the same from our world, we will have more freedom, more joy, more choice, and more peace. This is the ultimate reward of your warrior.

CHAPTER TWO

The Inner Workings
of the Warrior

*T*HE WARRIOR ENERGY LIVES inside each of us; it is as much a part of who we are as our ability to love, to feel, to think, and to dream. But for most of us, this warrior energy was put to sleep by the teachings of a culture whose goals have been based on manipulation and control. Since one who has owned his or her warrior cannot be controlled, it is not a quality that has been encouraged by society. Our entire education, beginning with our parents (even those with the best intentions), and including our schools and religious systems, has taught us who we ought to be, so that we fit the accepted mold, rather than supporting us to break the mold and be ourselves. We have been taught to be controlled rather than to have our own power.

Control is the need to manipulate something or someone because we are afraid of being overwhelmed. My own life provides me with the best examples for teaching this. Because of the way I grew up, very early on I became a control freak. I needed everything to be obedient to my will, including every piece of dust in our environment, so that I could be sure we were safe. I read every ingredient on every box or can of food before I let my little family eat it. I had a fit when I smelled Big Mac® on my daughter's breath. I hovered like a mother hen. It was exhausting, and it didn't work. My family members went on to create their own lives, make their own ways in a dangerous world. Learning to let go of them was one of my biggest lessons for letting go of control and the illusion that control would make us all safe.

The power of the warrior that we're exploring here comes from knowing that we create our world by our choices and by taking responsibility for those choices. Bringing forth the qualities of the warrior is essential at this time because in the warrior we find the antidote to tyranny and violence. We are a society addicted to violence and greed and it is the energy of the warrior that breaks addiction. As each individual takes responsibility for their own experience, finds their own path, cleans up their own mistakes, and lives their own truth, it becomes a better world. The warrior creates a safe place for us to live our lives, and without that, very little else has value.

As long as the warrior is identified with power over others rather than self-empowerment, following orders rather than trusting one's own truth, identifying an adversary and blaming others rather than taking responsibility, he or she is limiting his potentials to the qualities of a soldier, not a warrior.

We had a Vietnam vet come through one of our workshops who gave us a definition of the warrior's shadow qualities. He said that as a soldier he was expected to "suit up, show up, and shut up." There is a part of the self that my friend Animal, (yes, that's right, Animal), calls "combat computer." Combat computer is the part that got turned loose in Vietnam, that could level the landscape with no conscience or thought of the consequences, all moral law suspended. At its best it is Ramboesque, at its worst, it is the Terminator. In contrast to the soldier, the warrior respects life in all forms and holds himself or herself accountable for all his/her actions. It is this new paradigm that will safely take us to the 21st century, and that is what this book is about.

We'll be exploring four levels of warriorship, how they build on each other, and how they are interconnected. They are:

- *The Self:* Building your foundation
- *Relationship:* How we interact with other individuals
- *Community:* How we build our interactions with groups
- *Global:* How we nurture our relationship to the planet

$\mathcal{T}$HE SELF: BUILDING YOUR FOUNDATION

I believe that the basis for all other work is the work on the Self. A primary aspect of this is the ability to be responsible for our own personal safety, the right to self-protection. If you don't know that you can take care of yourself physically, you are always in a certain amount of fear, and that fear impacts your entire life. It affects the choices you make, the risks you take, and the goals you are willing to set. That fear literally defines how you are able to live your life. It doesn't matter how successful you are, how much therapy you've had, how good your meditations are, how great your relationship is, or how much you like your job; if someone can come along and take your life, all the work means nothing. Unless you know you are your own bottom line, you have no foundation from which to live your life, and everything in your world shifts around on you.

A natural part of our internal warning system, fear is designed to let us know when we are in danger, and to kick start our adrenals so that we are ready to deal with that danger—fight or run.

If you don't know how to protect yourself, that fear switch may be on all the time, which makes you unable to accurately read danger signals. You become vulnerable in the worst ways.

Self-protection is a basic and fundamental warrior skill. The physical body is an incredible gift from the Divine Mother. We know that it's only on loan, but while we are in it, we are responsible for it. Without it, we have no way to travel through our physical reality. The warrior's first responsibility is to protect the home he or she inhabits.

In nature there are three responses to danger: fight, flight, or close down. When the lion finally catches the gazelle, and the gazelle knows it is defeated and there is no escape from its own death, a freeze response kicks in that literally anesthetizes the gazelle. It simply doesn't want to be conscious while it's being lunch. I believe that in this society, we have been so conditioned to believe we can't take care of ourselves, our reaction to danger has been to shut down and submit. We have been brainwashed to think we have no choices. We submit not only to violence but to big business and big government or anything else that tells us it has more power than we do. No wonder we're depressed. Our society has done a very good job of teaching us this third option, and a poor job of teaching us about fight or flight. It's time to face the lion and fight for our lives, and our world. It's time to stand up to our tyrants even if we die, because if we don't stand up to them, we will die anyway.

The physical skills of self-protection act as a metaphor for the other areas of our lives. In teaching our workshops, I have noticed that wherever an individual needs work on their physical technique, that's where they usually need work in their life. For example, if a student has a problem closing the gap between themselves and a target, or a problem with distance, that may indicate an issue with closeness or intimacy. If someone's timing is off in their technique, their timing may be off in their life, as expressed in missed opportunities, chronic lateness, or acting precipitously. If they are afraid to let their physical power out, they may be afraid to go for their goals or their dreams or express themselves in other areas of their life. And in truth, most of us have been taught to fear our own power, to doubt ourselves and not to trust ourselves.

The physical body is an incredible map of our consciousness. If I see a student with their chest caved in, it usually means they are hiding their heart. If their upper body is held slightly back from center, it usually turns out they have a problem committing. If it's slightly ahead of center, they generally feel they need to jump the gun or they won't get what they want. If they lock their joints, they may be rigid in their lives. It's pretty simple if you just take the time to look, as any good body worker can tell you.

Some of the basic physical principles of warriorship can be understood in terms of how we make contact with the world and interact with it. While these principles are derived from martial arts training, they can be a metaphor for the other areas of our lives. They can help us understand our own style or approach to life. The following ten principles reveal much:

1. *Distance*

   Distance is the ability to set and stand up for personal boundaries. It is the ability to close the gap between oneself and an opponent, or oneself and a goal. It is the space between ourselves and anything or anyone else. Distance defines separation, or individuation. It makes it very clear that you are you, and I am myself. In the martial arts a warrior learns to recognize how much distance he or she needs to be "safe," outside the opponent's striking range but still within a range to take advantage of an opportunity to take one's opponent down. In our daily lives we recognize similar spaces, how close we'll allow a loved one, or how much distance we need between ourselves and strangers to feel comfortable. This applies to both physical and emotional boundaries.

2. *Timing*

   Timing is knowing when to strike, or when to act. In physical self-defense there is a half-second window that exists if someone is within striking range. If you act within this window and don't telegraph your move, you can't be stopped. With timing, it's important to understand both how to initiate action and how to respond.

   To initiate puts you in the position of being the one who starts an action. It means that an opponent has to operate in response to your move, responding rather than initiating, defensive rather than offensive. To initiate gives you the advantage of more choice. Good timing means you have to mentally close the gap between yourself and your opponent so that you can anticipate a move, or an idea. This is where the warrior uses his or her instincts or intuition to read intent prior to the moment the other person takes action.

3. *Balance*
   Balance is how we stand on Grandmother Earth, it is defined by how we feel our connection to Her. This can literally mean knowing how to stand so that we can move with maximum speed, power, and flexibility; or it can mean how we use and nurture the resources in our lives. As long as we honor the connection between ourselves and Grandmother Earth, putting back as much as we take, she will support us and we will be stable, solid, and grounded. Balance has to do with how respectful we are toward our own bodies and the world around us. Off balance, we are vulnerable, easy targets.

4. *Flexibility*
   Flexibility is finding more than one way to get the job done. It is fluidity, spontaneity, and the ability to move with and respond to changes. It is the willingness to change, to find a way over, under, or around the challenge you are facing if you can't find a way through it.

5. *Speed*
   Speed is how much time it takes to get from one point to another, to reach a goal, to close the gap. Though it might seem contradictory, speed comes from our ability to relax. When we're tense we contract our bodies and it constricts the flow of energy, like putting a crimp in a garden hose. Speed is more important than strength in self-defense technique;

whoever gets there first gets the job done. Speed is similarly important in how we respond to the present; fear, worry, or living in the past creates tension that insulates us from what's happening in the moment.

6. *Coordination*

   Coordination is how we organize movement in time and space. If it is organized effectively, we get the job done; if not, we get in our own way. There is an axiom that says, "The first Universal law is Order." Coordination is one of the attributes of order.

7. *Intent*

   Intent is purpose, resolve, the inner processes of will or volition. Intent is the energy of determining. Without intent, none of the other elements, distance, timing, speed, flexibility, etc., will work. With intent, you can take up any slack in the other elements. It is the warrior's most important weapon. The person left standing in a fight is usually the one with the strongest intent. One of the laws in the warrior's code, "Don't Quit," is a form of intent.

8. *Focus*

   Focus is the ability to bring one's attention and intention to one point in time and space. Focus is the point at which consciousness converges, concentrates, and becomes will.

9. *Power*

   Power is authority, freedom, choice, and the responsibility for that choice. However, most of us associate power with size, strength, or force. But what good is muscle mass if you're not fast enough to deliver the strike? Also, if you double the mass you double the power; if you double the *speed* you quadruple the power. What good is strength if you're not balanced enough to stay on your feet? What good is size if you're not coordinated enough to hit the target?

What good is weight if your timing is off and you
miss the mark? Each of these contributes to power.
There is an old samurai saying: "The sharpest
swords are never drawn." You never know what a
master knows until they need to use it. That's power.

10. *Breath*
The matrix of the entire system we are exploring
here is the breath. It is that which binds together all
of the other elements. It is our Chi, our Ki, our life
force, our intrinsic energy. Without breath, none of
the other elements will work. With proper use of the
breath, we find where our infinite resources are. In
the Bible, God breathed life into a lump of clay, and
it became man. By the same token, breath gives life
to the physical technique. It is the key (Ki), systole,
and diastole, expansion and contraction of the Universe. It is the secret that yogis and meditators, martial artists, and athletes have always known.

The Kia, which is the warrior's battle cry, uses the
breath to bring all of one's energy to one point in time
and space, and focuses and maximizes one's power.
The Kia also prevents the body from going into shock
when it's hit—it keeps the consciousness from disas-
sociating from the body. The Kia brings you, fully and
completely committed, into the present.

The use of the breath breaks the freeze response.
When we freeze, we stop breathing; without breath,
we can't act, we lose our life force. Proper use of the
breath accesses the place in us that knows how to
react to danger. That place is the warrior.

Primary Target Areas

As we consider the different aspects of self that come into
play in self-defense, it is important to know that there are certain parts of the human body that cannot be armored. These
are called primary target areas. We work with four, although

there are others. They are the eyes, throat, groin on a man, and knees.

If you are within striking range, and you initiate movement, don't telegraph your move, stay inside the half-second window, and strike a primary target area: you can't be blocked. You can drop anyone, I don't care how big they are.

Operating Keys to the Ten Principles

We teach that intent constitutes an attack. There are three kinds of intent:

- *Physical.* This refers to when someone is coming at you in a way that poses a real and present physical threat to you.

- *Verbal.* This refers to any vocal threat. However, these are to be taken seriously only when that threat can be executed. Empty threats don't count. If someone says, "I'm going to kick your ass!" from a block away, run. If they are close enough to follow through with the threat, strike.

- *Energetic.* This refers to the feeling in your gut when you know something's going down, the instinctual, internal warning system that lets you know when you are being threatened. Can you remember a time you felt your gut contract and realized you were in danger? Can you think of a time when you had a visceral reaction to another human being that told you to be careful? Can you think of a time when you ignored these internal warning signals and got in trouble? Our life energy emanates from three key centers of our body: the head center, the heart center, and the moving center in our belly. I'll be discussing these in greater detail in the next chapter. For now it is enough to know that how we use our energy is determined by the characteristics of each of these centers. For example, when we're thinking or reasoning, our energy is coming primarily from the head center. When we're engaged in a sport, our energy is coming from the moving center. And when we are experiencing our emotions our energy is coming from our heart center. We've been taught to trust the head center for all of our information, to the exclusion of the other centers, including our survival center. In a dangerous situation the head is too slow, it's always just a moment behind reality, meanwhile the belly brain or moving center is fully in the present. If you take your head into combat, the best it will do for you is comment while you get your butt kicked. The head center is the source of our projections of fear. The moving center or belly brain possesses the ability to accurately read danger signals and respond appropriately to them. The head center is where our self-doubt lives. The belly brain has no self-doubt.

We teach our students to trust their instincts, that the most effective response is to react when they read energetic intent, before the first strike is thrown at them.

One of the first things we teach is to always avoid combat if you can. Never pick a fight, never escalate a fight. Run away, talk it down, give them your wallet, give them your car. Your stuff is not worth fighting for; your ego is not worth fighting for. You fight only to defend yourself or another sentient being.

We also teach that if you do have to go into combat, you commit 100 percent, you don't stop until your opponent is no longer a threat. You go in with the attitude that today is a good day to die.

There are two sides to the development of the Self in warrior work. You have to know that there is no place in you that is willing to accept violence, to yourself, or any other sentient being. You have to know that there is no place in you that is willing to do violence. A warrior knows that the arrow cannot find its mark if there is no place to receive it.

The other component of first-level warrior skills besides physical self-defense is the warrior's willingness to look within, to turn our focus inward and see with clarity who we are and what we need to change.

In the psychotherapeutic process, it is the warrior who creates a safe container so that we may renegotiate old traumas whose memory may be limiting our lives.

It is the warrior self that empowers an incest survivor to let her inner child know that she is safe. Until we can stand up and say, "It will never happen again," the child that was wounded won't trust us to keep her safe. If an adult can't protect him or herself, how can they promise to protect a child? Once the inner child knows that the adult will go to the wall for her, do whatever it takes to keep her safe, the healing process can be complete. While your own sons and daughters look to your warrior for strength and safety until they have developed their own inner strengths, your inner child also looks to your warrior to keep him or her safe and free from fear.

The ability to face ourselves with honesty and compassion, and to change what we need to change, is a basic and essential warrior skill.

RELATIONSHIP: HOW WE INTERACT WITH OTHER INDIVIDUALS

To be able to create and enjoy an intimate relationship we need to know how to set boundaries with other people. Without boundaries, there is no respect, no sense of one's own autonomy, no sense of love freely given and received. If you know how to set boundaries, you don't have to build emotional walls. It's essential to be able to say, "This is my space, mentally, physically, emotionally, sexually, spiritually, and I have to give you permission before you can enter it." Without that, we have nothing that is ours and we have no self-esteem. Children who are abused have their boundaries stretched and trampled, and as adults, they often have a hard time setting them, feeling they have no right to ask for anything for themselves. They may become submissive victims or build walls around themselves so thick that having a relationship becomes impossible for them. Most children are treated like property instead of people, which conditions them to feel that they have no rights to their own boundaries.

Relationships can either accelerate the process of waking oneself up, or be used as an excuse to stay asleep. In a good relationship the partners are willing to ruthlessly (yet compassionately) mirror back to each other the parts of themselves that they might not see by themselves. A warrior does this without criticism or judgment, but in loving support of a partner's unfoldment. A warrior receives this with gratitude, knowing that in our willingness to be seen, we grow.

In a relationship, we agree as warriors not to collude. As warriors we never agree *not to see;* instead we agree to say what we see about our partner's habits or negative patterns. We don't keep silent about our partner's habits in exchange for not having to change our own. We agree that we are willing to see the truth and speak the truth, no matter how difficult it might be. We learn how ruthless dedication to the truth is sometimes the better part of compassion.

I think for most of us, love is the greatest risk of all. As warriors, we are willing to expose our hearts even knowing that there are no guarantees, simply because we love. We know that in loving one another we surrender, we give up our control, and risk the possibility of loss and pain. We also know that love gives our lives meaning, connects us to each other, and ultimately connects us to the Divine.

A warrior is not afraid of discipline, for ourselves or for our loved ones. In fact we view discipline as an integral part of our relationships. Those of us who grew up in families where discipline turned into abuse often find it difficult to discipline our children. We had no proper models. As warriors we know not to ask of another what we are unwilling to do ourselves. Discipline is not restriction or punishment; it is ultimately a move toward freedom. It is setting boundaries to establish a safe place. Children with no boundaries don't feel protected, secure, or cared for. And as adults we often carry these insecurities into our relationships. When you set a boundary for a child, they feel free to stretch to reach it. When they can safely fill that space, you renegotiate the boundary so that they can stretch some more. They learn the difference between freedom and license. They learn to respect themselves and others, and to trust themselves and others.

While there are issues and lessons we must learn to deal with as parents, most of us also need to deal with these same themes in our relationships with other adults. Often this means learning what we didn't get as kids. In a wolf pack, the community allows the cubs room to safely explore their environment and their own abilities. When they try to cross the line of safety, they are herded, or nipped back in. They learn to trust themselves to operate within a defined system, they learn to trust the adults to define that system. They intuitively know that if there were no limits set for them, they couldn't survive on their own.

Not setting boundaries for children is a form of abandonment, and whether we have children or not, we bring these issues from our own childhoods into our relationships. It is around these same themes of being clear about where we stand and recognizing the need for discipline in our lives that we learn to handle our fears of intimacy and open ourselves up to giving and receiving love in our lives.

*C*OMMUNITY: HOW WE BUILD OUR INTERACTIONS WITH GROUPS

The third level of warriorship is community: how we interact with our neighbors and our friends. How do we treat the garbage man, the old woman down the street with Alzheimer's, the grocery clerk, the cop who patrols our neighborhood, the homeless Vietnam veteran who has made our neighborhood his home?

What are you willing to do for the neighbor who is bedridden, about the neighbor who you know is abusing his kids, about the guy down the street who beats his dog? When are we willing to step in and when do we look away?

Native American's have a teaching that they give to their children at a very early age. They teach them that at some time, in one lifetime or another, everyone has been your aunt or uncle, a brother or sister, a mother or father, a cousin, a nephew or niece: so everyone should be treated as family. Most of the warrior skills we need for community are contained in that realization: that regardless of our judgments of others, we are truly One. In addition, we bring to community all that we have learned in building the foundation of Self and in the development of our close relationships.

GLOBAL:
HOW WE NURTURE OUR
RELATIONSHIP TO THE PLANET

The warrior knows that our planet is in trouble and does not try to deny or avoid the responsibilities this knowledge imposes on us all. We are wiping out our rain forests that provide us with oxygen, the prana or breath of the earth. We are blowing holes in the ozone layer, the aura or shield of the planet. Species of plants and animals are becoming extinct on a daily basis, gone, never to be seen again by our children or our grandchildren. We are wasting resources that don't belong to us and have effectively bankrupted our children. We are acting without respect. We are treating Grandmother Earth as if she weren't alive. We are committing suicide.

We are the most violent industrial nation on the planet. We have children in the inner cities with little chance of living happy and productive lives. There are more and more homeless people every day, more and more people hopeless and on drugs. We are witnessing genocide in several places on the globe. We are turning our back on the holocaust, after we had sworn never to allow it to happen again, or did that apply to one race only?

We need to wake up, stand up. The global warrior finds the part of him or herself that confronts tyranny and greed and violence. We need to confront it first in ourselves, and then turn and face outward to confront the tyranny on our planet.

The global warrior realizes that we have to wake up, that all four horsemen are loose. He or she knows that we cannot act as if what I do over here doesn't affect you over there. A global warrior knows we are all part of the same Self and as one person said to me, "We've got to stop peeing in the pool."

As global warriors we treat all things and all beings as if they were sacred, because they are.

The central premise of global warrior work is that each of us is all of it, the dark and the light, the good and the bad. We are each a microcosm of the macrocosm. We are responsible for ourselves and our world, because in the final analysis we are the world. Clearly the warrior's path is a spiritual path, a realization that is never clearer than when we contemplate our relationship to our planet. This is nothing less than the work of enlightenment.

When I first began my spiritual warrior journey, I wanted to skip the step of dealing with my own shadow stuff and go straight for God. I had my head in the clouds and my feet in the muck. You can't surrender what you don't own and the parts of myself I was unwilling to acknowledge because it was too painful or too hard, I found mirrored in my world. The parts of myself I denied kept showing up in my life in the form of resistance, or pain, or struggle until I learned not to fight them, but embrace them. I realized my life was big enough to include them, that they are all a part of me, in the same way we are all a part of God.

We are living in dangerous times, a pivotal time, a time when the choices we make will determine whether or not we survive as a species, whether or not we evolve as a species. Knowing this we ask, "How shall I choose?" It is our warrior that leads us to the place in ourselves where the choices are clearly revealed. "Do what thou wilt is the whole of the Law,"—Allister Crowley. "With harm to none," is the warrior's addendum.

*T*RY THIS

Take just one day and do an inventory. Begin when you first wake up and keep track of how you treat and use everything. Remember that the first law in the warrior's code is, "Pay Attention." Look at the toothpaste container: where did it come from? Where will it go when you're done with it? Notice the water running in your sink. Notice the food you eat—who, or what made it a gift to you? Was it given willingly or taken in fear? Before you put anything in your mouth, ask yourself if you could have harvested it yourself. Could you have killed the calf whose flesh is in the hamburger you're eating? Look at the newspaper, the plastic baggy, the can of cat food. Can what you use be replaced? If not, you are out of balance. One of the warrior's qualities is accountability. If you make a choice that's out of balance, at least notice it.

This is an exercise in mindfulness, or paying attention.

This is truly a loving and abundant Universe as long as we act with respect and gratitude and take responsibility for what we use.

CHAPTER THREE

Energy Centers

*T*HE WARRIOR WORK that I teach is based on some of the oldest existing metaphysical principles. These include: As above, so below; as within, so without. We are the microcosms of the macrocosm, the evidence of the Divine. The same way that we reflect the Divine, our world reflects us.

The process of becoming a warrior is essentially one of learning how to use energy. To be a warrior we need to know how energy is expressed in ourselves as well as how it is expressed by other people and the Universe. We need to know how we can best make use of energy for the benefit of all.

A simple example of why we need to understand energy and how we can use it to our advantage is found when we lift a heavy object improperly. If we don't know how to lift with our legs instead of our backs, we can cause damage to our backs by rupturing a disk or straining a muscle, or even fracturing a vertebra. To lift without injury, discomfort, or exhaustion, we need to understand basic principles about energy outside of us (gravity), and inside of us (body dynamics, how our bodies use the energy stored in the muscles, and how our skeletal systems work in relation to these energy factors). The simple understanding of physical laws, and the management of energy keeps us healthy and safe.

Many of you are already familiar with the idea that the universe is divided between two primary energy systems, masculine and feminine. Since we are *of the Universe*, we too have both these energies within us. In our exploration of the energies of the warrior, this seems like a good place to start.

The feminine energy principles are nonlinear, intuitive, inspirational, and spiritual. They represent our connection to Higher Wisdom: formlessness, all uncreated possibilities, the Mystery.

The masculine energy principles are linear, action-oriented, closely associated with will, manifestation, and form. It is the masculine energy which takes the inspiration (feminine) and gives it shape and substance in time and space.

Neither masculine nor feminine energies are more important or more powerful than the other. They are equals. They each possess different gifts, qualities, and powers. Together they are the Divine dance, the mystical marriage. Apart, they feel incomplete and yearn for each other. Separate they are limited; together they are limitless.

When any human being—man or woman—is balanced, there is an internal marriage of masculine and feminine. Both energies are in communication, in harmony with each other. "She" sources the idea; "he" makes it happen. The feminine within guides, and the inner masculine follows through. Neither controls because each honors the gifts of the other; they both have access to those gifts, and they recognize that together they complete each other. Since they willingly and freely share each other's gifts, they have no need to compete with each other.

Warrior work is about creating balance. This balance begins in ourselves. We start by establishing the inner balance of masculine and feminine energies. People who are out of touch with their feminine, intuitive, feeling, spiritual side, are soldiers, not warriors. They may be able to make things happen in the world, but they have lost their connection to others, and to Source. A soldier on the battlefield may be able to perform his job efficiently, but he is dependent on his superior officers, an authority outside of himself to tell him what to do. A warrior trusts his or her own internal knowing, and goes within for the truth.

Someone out of touch with their masculine side may be a great dreamer or nurturer, but they will have difficulty implementing their ideas and making things happen. They may have difficulty in backing themselves up, setting boundaries, taking action, and taking care of themselves physically. This is not a warrior, but a victim. Emerson said, "Nature has decreed that, whatever cannot defend itself, shall not be defended." Think of all the people you know who are afraid to go out alone at night, or walk in the woods by themselves, or go on their adventure. They depend on something or someone else to take care of them. They have placed their power outside of themselves. I believe that it's the widespread inability to take care of ourselves that has led to the use of guns and violence in this country. Lacking inner strength and self-trust, we look elsewhere than to ourselves for our safety. Anyone who has purchased a weapon for this reason knows that this doesn't solve the problem, and they still don't feel safe. One of the things we say to our students is, "If you don't have it in the shower with you, don't count on it." You've got to be your own bottom line.

If you reverse the natural order of allowing the feminine to guide, nurture, and inspire, and instead put the masculine energy in control, you soon run out of resources. You exhaust everything you have and eventually you come to a screeching halt because creativity, nurturing, new growth, and guiding the new growth are nonexistent.

In writing this book, there have been times when my conscious mind has said, "OK, that's it, we're out of ideas." At such times I pause, find my center with my breath, and remind myself that the ideas *come through me, not from me*. As soon as I get out of my own way, the ideas flow in again. When I remember the difference between taking credit or taking charge, versus taking responsibility, I don't run out of resources.

The warrior recognizes that in the world today, we have put the masculine in the controlling position and we are running out of resources. What we are seeing in terms of global upheaval, disaster, and earth changes is nothing other than Grandmother Earth reestablishing balance. With or without our cooperation, balance will be restored. Unless the laws that we live by are in alignment with natural law, they won't stand. The warrior knows that how we choose to support and work for balance will determine our future; it may even determine whether we have a future at all.

By holding the balance within him or herself, the warrior restores balance in the world. The warrior knows that you can't control power; you can only temporarily restrain it. The warrior knows that the only way to have power is to be in harmony with it.

THE ENERGY CENTERS

Part of warrior work is understanding how energy works so that we can properly manage it, and stay in balance. It is the management of energy within our own bodies that brings us into our own power and allows us to work in harmony with it wherever we are in life.

There are three primary energy centers in the human body: head center, heart center, and moving center (or belly brain). Each energy center governs specific areas of our lives. Each contains certain information and offers access to certain gifts. One of the objectives in warrior work is to get all three centers open, fully operative, and in alignment. Until they are, we are not fully functional, fully awake, or fully alive. We are not operating on all of our cylinders. One of the things the warrior has come through to do at this time is to wake us up to our full potential, and back us up as we claim that potential, turning possibilities into realities.

The Head Center

The head center is our intellect, our ability to think and reason. Our intellect serves us in many ways. The incredible advances of our technological society are gifts from our intellect. These gifts are supposed to make our lives easier. They are not supposed to separate us from our natural world but are intended to give us more time so that we can enjoy our lives. Comprehension, concentration, and focus all come from the head center. If we have access to the head center, we have the ability to strategize, plan, project our thoughts into the future, and understand the consequence of our actions over time. The highest function of the head center is wisdom, the understanding of Universal truth and Universal law, and man's relationship to those principles. The head center connects us to Divine Mind.

The Heart Center

The heart center is the seat of our feelings and our emotions. It is the ability to trust and love others. A warrior whose heart is awakened is able to experience the world around him as part of himself, to act with sensitivity and conscience, to be ruthless when appropriate, and forgive when possible. If the head center conceives the law, and the will enforces the law, it is the heart center which reminds us that love is the better part of the law. When we have access to the heart center we are inspired to come together in families and in community, to share our feelings, our dreams and our lives. The energy of the heart center gives us the desire to join with each other and unite with God. Love allows us to feel our connection to the All That Is.

The highest function of the heart center is compassion, which is nonattachment or love without any conditions. The heart center connects us to each other.

The Moving Center

The moving center, or belly brain, is our ability to act. This is the center of self-determination, will, sexuality, and the instincts of survival. The belly brain is the center in which the warrior spends most of his or her time. It is the instinctual self, and as the heart center gives us the ability to trust others, the moving center gives us the ability to trust ourselves. Although it is no more important than the other two centers, without it the other centers don't have a base from which to operate. It serves as the foundation for our lives since it is the seat of our survival. Someone who has access to their moving center is in touch with their instincts, their courage, their ability to take care of themselves, their willingness to take risks, and their sense of adventure.

The moving center is our power in the physical world, it is the ability to make things happen in time and space. The moving center connects us to the physical world.

The energy we know as human consciousness is composed of all three of these energy centers.

THE SUBCENTERS

Each of these primary centers contains subcenters. Each subcenter controls specific physical functions, including organs and glands. I was first introduced to this concept when I began to study yoga years ago. These centers are called *chakras* and have been known to Eastern physicians and metaphysicians for centuries. They are used in both their healing and spiritual practices.

The term chakra means "spinning wheel" in Sanskrit. Each chakra is symbolized by a specific color. The chakras are loosely organized along the spine, accounting for the power of the central nervous system to communicate with and integrate all the myriad functions of the physical self.

We work with seven primary chakras, although there are other, secondary ones. Only recently has information about them begun to filter into our empirical, allopathic Western healing system. Western healing has traditionally been based on physical data. It is just beginning to factor in the power of energy and consciousness in healing. We are starting to see systems such as acupuncture, homeopathy, the use of sound, the use of light, the understanding of the flow of energy in the body being used in conjunction with our medical technology. There has been a lot of resistance. After all, the AMA and the pharmaceutical companies have a lot to lose. They have attempted to legislate, and therefore get control of, most non-traditional healing systems. We're beginning to discover, however, that having access to both technologies contributes to our good health.

In discussing subcenters, or chakras, we will deal with only those concepts that are specific to warrior work as we teach it.

The Subcenters of the Head Center

There are two subcenters inside the head center.

The Seventh Chakra

At the top of the skull is the crown chakra, also called the seventh chakra. This center is open in a fully awake, enlightened human being. It connects individual mind to Divine Mind, since we are always connected to Source, whether we remember it or not. Warrior work is about learning how to fully experience that connection. This seventh chakra is the seat of transcendent awareness. It opens and we have access to its gifts only after we have learned to manage the energy of each of the six chakras preceding it. When we have moments of epiphany, we taste what it is like when this center is open all the time. Epiphanies give us perspective and hope, often occurring spontaneously during difficult times. They allow us to lose our sense of separation and serve to remind us that we are all part of something much greater than our individual selves. These moments inspired me to take the warrior's path so that I could find my way home.

The Sixth Chakra

The sixth chakra is located between the eyebrows. Some call it the third eye. It is the center of our ability to communicate nonverbally, our clairvoyance, our ability to see beyond the limits of time and space, and our sense of humor. We've all had experiences of knowing what someone was going to say before they said it. Or maybe you've experienced feeling as though you perfectly understood someone else, and what they were feeling, as though they lived inside of you. You may have had a feeling of timelessness, or of communicating with animals or nature. Have you ever felt like laughing at who we are and what we do, not from a place of ridicule, but from love. When we see our lives through our third eye we recognize that we are part of a plan far greater than ourselves, and the Creator of that plan has a sense of humor.

Subcenters of the Heart Center

There are two subcenters in the heart center.

The Fifth Chakra

The fifth chakra is located at the throat. This center is our voice in the world, our creative expression, the ability to speak our truth. It is our ability to give and receive, to ask for what we want and accept what we ask for when it is given. When this center is open, our relationships are full and rich. We allow free give and take. We speak our minds and our hearts. We hear what others say and mean. We are willing to share our stories as a way of healing ourselves and others. We are willing to share our gifts, and have our voice heard in our world.

The Fourth Chakra

Located near the heart, the fourth chakra is also called the heart chakra. It governs our feelings and emotions. It is our love for others, our desire for community. It is where we first experience compassion, which is love in its transcendent form. When our heart chakra is open, it opens our world. We are able to include others in our lives, to experience others, to let them in and allow them to be themselves. We are able to be ourselves and allow ourselves to be included by others. It is through heart chakra energy that we break down the belief in separation between ourselves and others, and ourselves and our world. It is the necessary ingredient in reclaiming the dark, lost parts of ourselves. It is how the warrior closes the gap between himself and an adversary, transforms the relationship, and turns the opponent into an ally. When the heart center is open we learn to trust others.

The Subcenters of the Moving Center

There are three chakras in the moving center, or belly brain. In the descriptions of the other chakras, we started from the top and worked down. We're going to change directions and start from the bottom and work up in the moving center.

First Chakra

At the base of the spine is the first chakra, or survival center. In this center energy takes form as everything we need to know to survive in the physical world. The same way as a mama lion knows how to care for and protect her young and herself, so do we. We have the same instincts hardwired into our system. We come into the world with them, and we always have them, although in humans, they are often suppressed. It can be useful to think of these instincts as being stored as energy in the first chakra. We may lose our connection to them, but they can't be eradicated.

When the energy and the instincts of the first chakra are suppressed, we cease to trust ourselves. If we don't know that we can survive in the physical world, then what does it matter what else we know? If we don't have the right to self-preservation, then what do we have? If we aren't safe, then what are we? Self-protection is a fundamental human right, and responsibility. People from whom it is taken are dependent on things external to themselves to take care of them (which is the classic definition of a victim) and can easily be controlled by people and events around them.

The Second Chakra

The second chakra, located between the pubic bone and the navel, is the sexual center. Our sexual and aggressive energy centers are on the same chakra. For most of us, the energy generated in the second chakra got shut down very early on. In virtually every social order there are disciplines and limitations placed on the expression of these drives. In the healthiest societies, both the individual and the community benefit from these disciplines. In our modern society, however, where control over others for the benefit of a few is a priority, we are taught to *repress* these second chakra instincts, or even use them to dominate others, not just to learn to discipline ourselves in their healthy expression. One of the primary ways modern society has controlled us is through the repression of this center, virtually closing down the energy we experience through it. If you can control someone's reproductive functions, you can almost completely control that person. If you can control their pleasure, you can make them your pawn. If you can produce guilt associated with these functions, you can destroy their self-esteem, and put them at your mercy.

It is important to recognize that the second chakra is also part of the survival system. This center contains our potential for reading intent and for reading the emotional climate. Together with the first chakra it lets you know when you are in danger, contributing much to your internal warning system. Fear, in its appropriate function, lives here as part of your warning system. If the second chakra is shut down, you don't have access to that critical information; you can't tell when you are in danger, and this makes you vulnerable. When this is the case, unconsciously you know this, and your fear switch is on all the time, running the adrenals overtime and poisoning the physical and emotional self. When you're living in that high adrenaline state, you're jumpy, stressed out, anxious, on edge, distrustful, and even a little paranoid. Sound familiar? Adrenaline is a gift from the physical self to spring you into action when you are in danger. It puts the body on overdrive, making you faster, stronger, more aggressive, and more impervious to pain. But the body can only safely metabolize small doses. More than a little is toxic.

The Third Chakra

The third chakra, located just above the navel, is will, self-determination, and action. It is the center that in a threatening or dangerous situation gathers information from the first two centers and acts on it. It is awareness of self in relationship to the world around us. This is the center that manifests, that makes things happen. When this center is shut down we don't trust our instincts, we don't go on our adventures, and we don't make our contribution to our world.

These three chakras comprise the moving center. The moving center is where the warrior lives. It is the part of the self that is fully present and engaged with reality. Unlike the conscious mind, which is one beat behind any action taking place in the present, the belly brain is completely in the present. It is in the now, fully aware, fully awake, and fully committed to appropriate action.

Unlike the head center, it has no self-doubt. When it is awakened, it trusts itself and acts on what it knows. Unlike the heart center, it is free of emotional content, including anger, attachment, grief or fear in their inappropriate form. It knows that emotions can cloud the senses, interfere with right action, alter perceptual awareness, put you off balance and ruin your timing.

When one operates from the belly brain, it is a state of awareness that is primordial and pure. When this center is open, we trust ourselves; when it is not, we cannot.

Other Chakras

There are also minor chakras in the hands and feet. Someone with the ability to heal has the chakras in their hands active and open. Their hands often heat up when they work on someone.

The chakras in our feet connect us to Grandmother Earth. We pull energy up from Her, through the soles of our feet, and store it in our bellies. The next time you are tired or know you are going to need some reserve energy, find a place outdoors where you can stand on earth or grass and take off your shoes. Dig your toes in, feel your connection to the ground, put your awareness where your feet meet the earth. Inhale and pull energy up through the soles of your feet, through your legs and into your belly. Do this exercise until you feel heat in your belly.

Many Native American dances employ a certain foot movement that looks almost like shuffling. The purpose is to connect with the earth, to feel her skin, to let her know we are here.

The most important teaching contained in the understanding of the energy centers is to see how we are given everything we need. In other words, we have all the intelligence, all the love, and all the power we will ever need. These gifts are all contained in the energy centers. Initially, they are available to us, and although they may be suppressed, the potential is always there. Warrior work is about recognizing which of our centers are awake, and which ones we need to awaken to be fully in our power. It is about what we must do to reclaim that power.

*W*ARRIOR BREATH

Learning how to breathe properly is the first thing you'll need to do to energize the centers we've just described. The breath is the matrix of our system.

Proper use of the breathe literally moves the energy wheels we call chakras. Improper use of the breath prevents the chakras from moving. Warrior breath is nothing very mysterious. The fact is that it is the way we human beings were designed to breath naturally. Because of the stress in our daily lives, however, we have forgotten how to breathe properly. We tend to take shallow breaths and when we are under stress or when we're in fear we hold our breath, which immobilizes us and cuts us off from our life force or vital energy. Notice how a baby breathes. Watch how the belly moves with each breath. This is how the body was designed to breath and it provides us with a model for the warrior breath.

$\mathcal{T}$ RY THIS

For this exercise, stand with your feet shoulder-width apart, shoulder over hip, knees soft, head and neck straight. Tuck your pelvis slightly forward to bring your spine into alignment. Relax. Place one hand on your chest and one on your belly. Begin by noticing how you are breathing. What moves as you inhale? Let your belly be soft and with your next breath, fill your lungs. Let your belly expand like a bellows on the inhale. When you exhale, use your belly to expel the air. Let your chest be as still as possible, filling your belly first when you inhale, then filling your upper body. Then empty your belly by contracting your abdominal muscles. Let your breath be slow and steady. After a few moments, notice if your awareness changes. Practice this until it becomes natural again. If you find yourself in stress or fear, notice how you are breathing. Change to warrior breath and see how your experience shifts.

You will find your transition back to natural/warrior breath fairly easy. Your body will work with you to regain its power by unlearning old habits and coming back to the patterns that are built into it.

*S*OFT FOCUS

Soft focus is another skill we teach early on in the workshop. It is a way of using your vision to expand your awareness. We normally focus on one object at a time, in a fairly narrow field of vision. Soft focus opens our field of vision and enhances our perceptual awareness.

*T*RY THIS

For this exercise, sit or stand someplace where you can be quiet and attentive to the exercise. Select an object across the room and focus on it. Concentrate hard on that one point in space. Then relax your eyes and stop focusing on the object. Soften your focus until everything becomes slightly diffused. If you have difficulty doing this, try looking out of both corners of your eyes, or looking slightly cross-eyed. Notice how your field of vision opens. Your peripheral vision should be greatly expanded, your awareness of movement enhanced, and you should have a sense of heightened awareness of everything around you. Switch back and forth from soft to hard focus until it becomes easy.

An additional exercise is to stand opposite someone, about three or four feet apart. Using the other person's sternum as a point of reference, go into hard focus on that point and notice how much you can see. What are the limits of your visual range, up and down and peripherally? Switch to soft focus using the same point on the sternum. Again notice your visual range. How much more of your partner's body can you see when you are in soft focus as compared to hard focus? If done correctly, your field of vision will be greatly increased and you will be able to take in much more visually.

One of our students in Michigan was applying for a civil service job as a forest ranger, kind of a critter cop, which was perfect for her because of her love and understanding of animals. She was taking an exam, one part of which involved looking at a picture for two minutes, then putting the picture away and answering questions about what she saw. She had to do this with two different pictures. The first time she studied the picture and tried to memorize as much as she could. When it came time to answer the questions she said she did fairly well.

The second time, she got an inspiration; rather than trying to memorize anything, she would simply go into soft focus and look at the picture. This time when she had to answer the questions about what she saw, she did great. By using soft focus, she was able to take in and retain much more information. As we relax, open up, and allow the energy to move through our bodies, which is exactly what these exercises do, we get our chakras moving. In the beginning they may move only a little, but as we continue to practice, they will continue to open and move. The purpose of these exercises is to give us an experience of what it feels like to have our chakras energized. We begin to have a sense of our own vitality, what it is like to be fully present in our bodies. It is a way to build our awareness of our warrior self. If at first the results seem sporadic—much of what we experience at the beginning is at a subliminal level—employ your warrior skill of self-discipline, and soon you will see a change, perhaps subtle at first, in the clarity with which you see your world.

As we become more adept and aware of the energy in various parts of our beings, we might begin to recognize tension around the throat chakra which may mean we are feeling the need to express ourselves. Or we may find tension or even aching in our heart chakra, suggesting that we have an unhealed wound in that area. As we begin to listen to the messages that our bodies give us we become aware of the old wounds, or present issues, that need our attention. The warrior acknowledges this feedback, takes it in, and trusts the information. How we address this phenomenon is the subject of the next chapter.

CHAPTER FOUR

Identifying the Wounds

WARRIOR WORK IS ABOUT taking our power back in the areas in which it has been diminished or taken away. It means getting our energy centers open and balanced, working in harmony and in an integrated way. We begin by identifying the centers that are not open. An important part of warrior work is understanding how these centers got shut down, and opening them up again so that we have access to their gifts. We renegotiate our past by taking our power in our present.

Each of us, as a child, is wounded in at least one of the three key energy centers, the head center, the heart center, or the moving center. Most of us have wounds of some kind in all of the centers. In spite of these numerous wounds, there is usually a primary wound. When it is identified and healed there is often a chain reaction that brings awareness and healing to all the other areas where we may be wounded. The work of renegotiating our past, healing our wounds, and changing limiting, habitual, or destructive behavior, begins with locating where we were wounded. Only when we can identify this area can we go back in to heal it. Until healed, each of our wounds weakens us or makes it difficult for us to recognize or access the power of our warrior self. The warrior knows that who we are is bigger than anything that can be done to us.

Even during the times when we cannot hear the warrior's voice or experience its power, that voice continues to speak within us until in spite of our wounds, we do begin to hear. The role of the warrior is to create a safe container for us to do the inner work that is our healing. The warrior gives us the courage to face our fears and make a commitment to change. The warrior waits for just the right moment to emerge to make itself known to us. I have experienced this occurring in my own life many times, but I have also seen it happen again and again with our students in our workshops.

Most of you have experienced moments of extraordinary strength, or insight, or feeling, beyond who you believed you were, or beyond what you were taught you could do, or beyond what you thought you could know. In spite of our wounds, our warrior shows up for us in times of our greatest need, often in unexpected ways. For this reason it is important to take particular notice of such events, to acknowledge them as the presence of the warrior in your life.

*F*INDING THE WOUND

Where the pain lives is where the wound is; however, it's not always easy to locate the pain. The consciousness, in order to avoid the pain, tends to move to and live from another center, perhaps even numbing the area that really hurts. In many ways our consciousness is like a child with a new box of crayons. If that child is given a full palette of colors to play with, but gets smacked every time she goes to pick up green, pretty soon she won't use green and eventually she might even forget it exists. In the same way, if every time the consciousness tries to access or express information from one of the energy centers, it gets zapped, or experiences pain, it will stop going to that center.

Each of the centers is wounded in a different way. For example, a critical or judgmental parent can create a wound to the head center, affecting the sixth and seventh chakras. Or these wounds might involve your being treated as if you are not too bright; or being ridiculed because you are bright; or being warned, as many women were in childhood that it isn't attractive to be too intelligent. If you are wounded in these ways you'll usually turn your attention to one of the other centers. You might run your energy from one of the other centers, at least until such a time that it is safe to reclaim your intelligence.

If a parent lies or breaks trust with you, that is a wound to the heart. A heart wound can also involve a parent's refusal or inability to care for a child's emotional needs, or to validate the child's own feelings. A parent's refusal to acknowledge a child's true gifts, to see who they really are can be extremely damaging to this energy center. The parents who insist that their children become something other than who they really are, that they abandon their own dreams to fulfill the dreams of the parents, cause a heart wound. For example, while exploring his early wounds, one of our students realized that his very financially successful career in business was really the career his father had never had, and not what our student really wanted. He was living his father's dream and not his own: he had suppressed his own potential in order to be the person his father wanted him to be. Each child is a unique and individual expression of the Divine, and a parent's job is to support each child to develop their true potential. Not to do so is a breach of trust.

Betrayal is a heart wound, as is emotional blackmail and withholding affection or approval. Children of alcoholic parents who have to become parents for the adults, and those who, for any reason, become the responsible family member at an early age, also sustain heart wounds.

Abandonment is a belly brain wound. A child instinctively knows that if a parent neglects its basic physical needs, it will die. Physical survival is our most primitive instinct. To be wounded on that level can result in deeply entrenched fear. Look at all of the parents who have walked away from their children and you'll begin to get a glimpse of one reason why fear is so rampant in our culture. Sexual abuse is also a belly brain wound. Incest, because it is both a sexual wound and betrayal, usually wounds both the belly and heart centers.

For the simple sake of survival, our psyches naturally shift from a center where there is pain, to one of the other centers where it feels safer. The person then experiences their life from there. So we often see that a person with deep wounds may have highly developed skills in one area with minimal abilities in another. For example, an individual might be very skilled in their work, generous and nurturing to others, but unable to develop an intimate relationship. Or someone might be a computer genius, but have a hard time communicating with others, and be unable to make things happen in their world. Someone might amass a fortune but never let themselves express their own feelings, or experience the feelings of others.

The obvious detriment is that we are cut off from our wholeness. We are literally missing huge pieces of ourselves.

When we first moved to Marin, I invited my new friend, Donna, to join one of my workshops. I had met her at my gym. She was an aerobics instructor and former dancer. She had great grace, strength, agility, and freedom of movement, so I was certain she'd be a quick study in learning the physical technique. She is also an incredible healer and is the person I go to when I need hands-on work.

As soon as we began the physical part of the workshop and I began teaching the combat stance, which is a defensive position, her body literally caved in on itself and assumed the posture of a child protecting itself from a beating. I was shocked and so was she. She was working in front of a mirror and I said, "Look at yourself," and there, looking back at her, was her little girl, waiting for the first blow. Throughout the workshop, little by little, she was able to release the old memory from her body, as she demonstrated to her little girl that there was now an adult who could take care of her. Slowly, her posture changed. Finally, during the combat portion of the workshop, she literally picked Robert up and slammed him to the mat. It was a tremendously powerful breakthrough experience, not only for Donna, but for everyone there, demonstrating the great power of the healing process.

That frightened little girl had lived in her body's memory waiting until she knew it was safe to reveal herself. In the process, the past was healed for her.

It is no accident that part of the work Donna does helps people release body memory so that they can return to a natural healthy state.

HEALING THE WOUNDS

While the prospect of healing old wounds can be difficult and sometimes frightening, the warrior work I describe here makes the process clear and straightforward.

The first step is to identify for yourself where your primary wound lives. Begin by acknowledging the parts of yourself you have owned. These are the gifts and talents you have already realized. You can use them as your base as you reclaim the ones you have lost access to. A warrior understands that part of good strategy is knowing what resources are available, and using them to get what he or she wants. What are you good at? Are you sensitive or nurturing, in touch with your feelings and emotionally available for others? Are you willing to speak your truth, ask for what you want and accept it when it's given? These are qualities of the heart center. This center also gives you your voice in the world, makes you able to speak up for yourself and others. You may be someone who will break the conspiracy of silence about all of the abuses that take place all of the time against our children, minorities, animals, and our natural resources. Perhaps because of your ability to love, to experience your feelings and emotions, you will help to build a bridge over the fear that separates us. These are spiritual warrior qualities that are badly needed at this time.

Are you courageous, willing to take risks, instinctual, elemental, fierce in the protection of yourself or your loved ones? These are qualities contained in the moving center.

The first chakra, or root chakra, found in the moving center is aptly named because it is the foundation in the physical self. If you have access to this chakra you may be someone others can trust as they learn to trust themselves. If your second chakra is open, you may have a heightened awareness of your surroundings, an ability to read danger, and perhaps lead others through dangers until they can make their own way. If you have the gift of courage, the willingness to face your own fears, the ability to stand up to tyrants, a sense of purpose, of being a part of something bigger than yourself, you are someone who is grounded in the moving center. This is the source of your strength and skill. These are the parts of yourself you can depend on. You can draw from the personal resources you have as you go on to open up the other areas in yourself that you wish to develop further.

Are you intellectually quick? Do you learn things easily, teach things well, have the ability to reason, to grasp with your mind? Can you see the order behind the appearance, the logic behind the law, the law behind the logic? These are all qualities of the head center. It is the people with strengths and abilities in this area that are helping to develop the strategy to save our world. They are the ones who can understand the Divine plan and help us create plans for taking action in alignment with it.

Concentrate on each center in your self, one at a time, and as you do, place your hands on that center, and think of all of the gifts it contains.

Honor the gifts that you do have. Think about how your life has been made better as a result of them. Embrace these parts in yourself, thanking them, blessing them. As you do so also respect the place in yourself that knows when you are ready to go after the parts that are temporarily lost.

Notice the people around you. See if you can identify which chakras or key energy centers seem to be strongest for them and which are yet to be developed. Notice which parts you have the most difficulty identifying. This is usually an indication of the areas we need to work on in ourselves. If, for example, you have a particular aversion to people who appear weak or helpless, with some honest introspection you may find they are mirroring back to you the vulnerable part of yourself you are afraid to express in your life.

Whatever we are cut off from in ourselves we can't share with others, so everyone is denied the gift. If my creativity got shut down, I am denied the joy of creating, and you are denied the experience of the creation. What if Mozart's mother told him he was no good at the piano?

Many of us feel inhibited about sharing our greatest gifts; we question their value and how they will be received. But the truth is, the most generous and loving thing we can do, for ourselves and others, is give and express these gifts fully.

Notice how groups of people are affected collectively. What if we convinced an entire race they were not too bright, and refused to educate their children because we said they couldn't learn? Imagine what we might lose, what gifts that could have been shared by all the world would be lost. The African Americans in this country have suffered through generations of being treated collectively as incapable of intellectual development. Sociologists tell us there is absolutely no basis for this belief, that this thinking grew out of the need for slave owners and traders to dehumanize African Americans in order to rationalize the abuse of the slaves. Out of this wound has come a shift to the moving center. As a result, as a group they tend to run primarily belly brain energy. Our prisons are filled with young African American men; our welfare rosters are filled with African American women. We bought the lie and we are all paying for it. On the positive side, many great athletes, dancers, and musicians have evolved as a result of this emphasis on moving center energy. They in turn have inspired others in this group to go on and develop and express the skills and abilities associated with the head center, which had been held down by prejudice and fear.

Women in our society have tended to run primarily heart energy. Most have been taught that they are helpless and as a result many have been victimized economically and sexually. These are wounds to the moving center, where our power and our sexuality live. The feminine has been under attack on this planet, as evidenced by violence against women in all its forms: from inequality in the workplace to the destruction of

our natural resources, which are associated with Grandmother Earth. As women, individually and collectively we
are finding our power center, and are standing up to our
tyrants internal and external. As this continues to happen,
the world around us is changing, becoming more respectful of
the feminine, and nurturing and supportive of the rights of all
living things.

Most men in our society have been taught to fear their
emotions, so they operate primarily out of their head center.
The heart also contains the conscience, so not only have
many men been cut off from their feelings, they have also
been able to behave in ways that disregard both short and
long-term consequences to others. How else can we explain
big corporations, and big government, the last bastions of
male supremacy, continuing to trash our environment and
exploit all our resources for their own personal gain. The Jewish people at one time operated primarily out of the head and
heart centers and found themselves almost destroyed because they couldn't access their survival center. They easily
fell victim to the Nazi regime, in part for this reason. As they
awakened this survival center, they went forward to create
Israel, their own country, now a major force in the world.
Israel is an example of what happens when you heal the
wounded center. The Israelis are incredible warriors. Their
warriorship has developed not just in the moving center, but
in the continued evolution of their head and heart centers as
well. Their head center is expressed through their world leaders and political strategizing; their heart center is expressed
in their development of community and family while encouraging the gifts of each individual.

TRY THIS

Activating Your Belly Brain

So how do we begin to reclaim what we have lost touch
with? The short answer is that we *pay attention*. In our work,

we first ground our students in their moving center since we consider this to be our base; it is the place where the warrior lives.

The other two centers are equally important, but the moving center guides us through our world, safely negotiating reality, fully engaged and fully present. Living from the belly means being in the moment, which is all there ever is. While the other two centers also continue to function at all times, they do not override the belly brain. The belly brain is the point man; he gets there first and tells the rest of the troops if it's safe.

To get in touch with your belly brain, get quiet, making sure that you are using your warrior breath (page 38). Sit so that you are comfortable and completely relaxed. Check your body for tension. To do this, scan your body with your awareness, starting with the top of the head and moving all the way down to your toes. You may want to tense and relax each set of muscles to get a sense of how tense or relaxed you are in each area. Wherever you are holding tension, with your next exhalation, let it go. Imagine your breath going directly to that place, visualize the area getting soft and flexible. Continue to do this until you are relaxed and have released, with your breath, all tension in your body. Now close your eyes or go into soft focus. Bring your attention into your belly, focusing approximately halfway between your navel and your pubic bone. Breathe into your belly with long, slow, steady breaths, letting your belly be soft. Fully expand your belly on the inhale, and empty it on the exhale, slightly exaggerating your warrior breath. Just notice what you feel there. Memory is stored in our bodies and that includes all kinds of valuable information regarding old wounds. Keep your awareness in this center, focus on your belly rising and falling with each breath. If your attention starts to drift, perhaps going over things that happened in your day, or what you think you should be doing instead of this, gently bring it back to the present. Notice what you feel. Is there resistance or anxiety? Stay with the process and especially notice if your conscious mind tries to pull you away. Any time you notice your attention drifting, gently bring it back to your moving center. Pay attention. Do you feel sadness, grief, fear, or anger? Simply notice, and let yourself experience what you feel. Just allow yourself to *be* with it, without having to *do* anything with it. This process may take a few times, but this is perfectly normal. Just keep doing it. Eventually, your body will release its secrets to you. You may have an old memory come up, or feelings about something that you didn't even know was there, or have an insight into why you have developed a certain behavior. Whatever comes up, simply stay with it with your awareness, and follow it with your breath. You may find that behind that feeling is valuable information.

I used this exercise to help me understand my fear of success. I followed the resistance in until it opened, and on the other side of it I found my fear of being seen by anyone other than those closest to me. Using my breath I followed that in until it opened and I discovered the old belief that being seen meant exposing my soft heart to strangers, who would then know I really wasn't a bad-ass. It was my fear of vulnerability left over from my childhood when I had to hold the line against danger. Behind all that I finally experienced the understanding that love is the only power, and it is the source of my power. And I can still be a bad-ass, but only when I need to.

Expanding Your Field of Awareness

The next exercise is about teaching ourselves how to take in more of our world with our senses. It is a way to let in more information about what is happening around us; it allows us to include more in our perceptions and be more aware.

Find someplace outside in nature where you can walk. Go into soft focus: be sure you are using your warrior breath, and begin to walk. Notice how your awareness changes. Your field of vision will open up. Colors are brighter, senses are enhanced. Notice how your hearing and your sense of smell become sharper, and how much more aware you are of movement. If you are breathing correctly and stay in soft focus it will drop you into your instinctual self. Notice how much more connected you feel to everything, how much more in the present you are. Now shift into hard focus and change to shallow breathing and see how your world closes down.

Try this exercise a few times until you are comfortable with it. Then try the same exercise walking through a crowd. Walk down the street or through a mall using the same technique, in soft focus and with your warrior breath. See how much more aware you are of everything and everyone. Many times when we have our workshop groups do this exercise, they describe how they suddenly become aware of a much bigger picture, instead of experiencing their world through tunnel vision.

With growing awareness of both the external world and our internal life, we become increasingly attuned to our own gifts and strengths as well as how we can build upon them. We also become more aware of where our energies are shut down, allowing us to focus and seek out ways to reawaken them. This growing awareness is, in fact, what the warrior's path is all about. It is a path that is best understood as an ongoing process, guided by the opening of our total being to life.

CHAPTER FIVE

Boundaries
and Territories

*I*F YOU WERE TO OBSERVE a mama lion in nature you would see that she is very territorial. She will do whatever she feels she needs to do to protect her boundaries. She may even seem vicious and violent, but this behavior comes from an instinctual center, knowing that this protection and definition of her boundaries is essential not only to her own survival, but to the survival of her kind. She is an excellent model for us on one of the key principles of warriorship, that is, the issue of boundaries and territories.

It is worth noting that the inability to establish boundaries, protect them, and respect them in others is widespread in our society. It is a reflection of early wounds to the first three chakras, one or all of them, making it difficult for us to own the moving center.

In everyday life boundary issues may come out as an inability to say no to people who make demands on us, or it might come out in an inability to say yes, or to allow anyone else into our lives. There is hardly an area in our lives where boundaries aren't involved, whether it's driving on the freeway, communicating your needs to your partner, or disciplining yourself to learn something new.

warrior work, it's important to first establish your ~~ical~~ safety. This can start even before you have ~~a. ressed~~ the issues that created your inability to set and stand up for your boundaries in the first place. One of the principles we teach about boundaries in our workshop is the five-foot law. A distance of five feet between yourself and another human being puts you out of normal striking range. Striking range is determined by the length of the longest weapon, which is normally someone's legs. If you meet a potential opponent whose legs are longer than five feet, adjust the distance (and call the NBA). If you are in unfamiliar territory, or uncomfortable with someone, maintain the five-foot boundary. There is a prison term, "Give me five feet." It means, give me enough space to feel safe. Maintaining this distance does two things: it gives you room to maneuver and it also respects the boundaries of the other person. Just as you may be uncomfortable with someone inside that space, so might they, and it could unnecessarily provoke aggressive behavior.

I believe that first establishing physical safety (by establishing and standing up for our boundaries in physical space) accelerates the process of learning to set boundaries in the other areas of our lives. Remember, there are mental, emotional, sexual, and spiritual boundaries, but they all share common principles for recognizing and working with them.

Setting a boundary isn't going to do you much good if you can't stand up for that boundary. Someone is going to cross that boundary. Were mama lion to fail to do whatever it takes to preserve her boundaries she wouldn't have any place to be. But once having established her boundaries, and her willingness and ability to defend them, she is not often challenged. After all, a lion at rest is still a lion.

I strongly believe in the importance of each individual learning physical self-defense skills. If everyone was able to take responsibility for their own personal safety, there would be far fewer places for violence to be expressed. I do not believe these skills can be taught in a book or even by videotape. One must find a good teacher and get hands-on training.

So, any of the physical principles I discuss in this book come with the disclaimer that they do not take the place of a good self-defense class.

Without boundaries there is no safe place for us to live our lives. We have little or no self-esteem and no self-respect, no sense of our right to our own feelings, and no sense of our right to our own lives. When Robert Frost said, "Good fences make good neighbors," he was talking about boundaries.

We've all seen parents who don't know how to set boundaries with their kids. These kids in turn have no respect for anyone else's boundaries.

We've seen women who have no boundaries with their husbands, men who have no boundaries with their wives. They do whatever the other wants and pretty soon they have no life of their own.

A boundary is when we say, "Not against my will, not without my consent. If you want it, I must freely give it. I must willingly receive whatever you want to give." Setting boundaries is when we say, "This is my space. I must give you permission to enter it, or you shall not enter. And I have the right to withdraw that permission whenever I choose." It is when we are willing to say, "These are my thoughts, my feelings, my desires. I can choose to share them with you or not, and I don't change them for anyone."

YOU HAVE A RIGHT TO YOUR SPACE

There is a certain amount of space that we occupy as human beings. It belongs to us for as long as we are in a physical body, and like our physical body, we are responsible for it. That space is defined by our aura. An aura is an energy field projected by the physical self. It changes size and color depending on one's emotional state. It is visible to people with developed psychic abilities, and can be photographed, or measured electronically, to satisfy those with empirical needs.

The halo depicted in religious pictures is the aura, although one doesn't have to be a saint to have one; everyone has one. It can operate as a shield, or protective filter against negative energy, so it is part of the self-protection system. The aura is the first energetic boundary, literally produced by the body's electromagnetic and acoustic radiation.*

Since your energy field is your portable home in the Universe, anyone wishing to enter that space needs to ask permission. There is tacit, ongoing permission in families, between lovers, parents and children, and friends, but permission must be given and not assumed. Permission can always be withdrawn or renegotiated. Not having dominion over this boundary, or control over this space results in a loss of a sense of self. If you don't have this, then what in the Universe is yours? When a person is trying to control another, they often will attempt to breach this boundary as a way of dominating and imposing their will on the person whose boundary they've breached. One of the first things we support our students to do is become aware of this boundary, and take responsibility for it.

*U*SING YOUR VOICE TO SET BOUNDARIES

Learn to use your voice to set boundaries. The voice carries intention. Begin by remembering you have not only the right, but the responsibility to protect your boundaries. When you use your voice, you don't *ask*, you *tell* someone to respect your boundaries.

---

* See "The Scientific Basis for Healing with Subtle Energies," by Glen Rein, Ph.D., Quantum Biology Research Laboratory, Palo Alto, Ca. Report published in *Healing With Love*, by Leonard Laskow, Wholeness Press, Mill Valley, 1998, pages 289–319.

One of our recent graduates gave us an example of using the voice as a boundary. Susan was running by herself in the hills a couple of weeks after completing the workshop. A car with three guys in it passed her. The car turned around and passed her again. The car stopped just ahead of her and three guys got out. Susan stopped running, stood her ground, faced the guys and said in a loud, clear voice, "I don't know what you think you're doing, but you get back in the car and stay away from me!" All three stopped in their tracks and backed away. Then, in a shaky voice, one of them said, "Please, lady, I live here. Honest!"

Embarrassed, Susan apologized, turned away, then continued her run. But as she ran, she also realized that she had stopped these guys cold. They recognized she meant business, whether it turned out to be a mistake or not. Above all, it was great practice since nobody got hurt.

$\mathcal{T}$RY THIS

Defining Your Space

There are a couple of simple exercises you can do to begin getting a sense of your personal space and what it can feel like to defend it.

Stand with your feet shoulder-width apart, soften your knees, and relax your upper body. Feel your connection to Grandmother Earth by consciously placing your awareness at the point where your feet meet the ground. Now bring your attention into your belly by using your warrior breath. Extend both arms in front of you, arms and fingers straight. Inhale, and as you exhale, slowly move your arms outward, using your breath to fill the circle defined by your arms. Inhale again, and on the exhale, imagine the circumference completely around you, with you at the center. Imagine that you are standing in a cocoon of energy the same distance from any point on your body as the space around you that you have defined with your outspread arms. With each breath, fill that space as it extends above you, below you, behind you, and in front of you. Scan your awareness. Does it have any color? How do you feel standing inside it? Do this exercise until you begin to have a tangible experience of this energy field.

In the next exercise, find someone to work with that you trust. Work in a carpeted room or an area where your partner can move silently. Cover your eyes with a blindfold and put earplugs in your ears. Stand in a relaxed position, feet shoulder-width apart, knees soft, upper body relaxed, hands gently resting on your thighs. Your partner's job is to approach you slowly and get as close as they can. Your job is to be aware of the approach. As soon as you sense that they are inside your aura, say, "Stop." It may take some practice before you reawaken this part of your awareness. Do this exercise until you are consistent in your ability to read the approach. The next step is to gradually increase the distance until you are able to extend your awareness up to five feet.

Many years ago I was teaching a workshop in Portland, Oregon. One of my students was a woman who was legally blind, and in the process of completely losing her eyesight. She wanted to travel before she lost her vision entirely, and took the workshop so that she could feel safe doing so. She worked hard all weekend, and was as prepared as anyone else in the workshop when it came time for the combat portion of the workshop at the end of the day on Sunday. She did her first two rounds in normal daylight, which would approximate twilight to a normal-sighted person. For her final round, I turned the rheostats down on the lights, so that for the normal sighted, it was like twilight, but she couldn't see. I had both of the attackers work with her at the same time. They began very slowly, approaching her from different directions with different attacks. Her response was clumsy at first, as she learned to trust her other senses, including her aura. Gradually, her responses began to shift, and she began to anticipate the direction the attack was coming from, and the speed with which it was delivered. The attackers began to move with more speed and power, and she turned to meet each attack with more confidence. As the energy escalated, it was like watching an incredible dance. Before the round was over, the attackers came at her with full force and intention, and she met each attack before they could lay a hand on her. When it was over, there wasn't a dry eye in the place, including mine.

As you go through your day pay attention to how you handle boundaries. Notice where you feel comfortable or uneasy in proximity to others. You might notice that there are particular situations where boundaries are disregarded, such as on a crowded bus where people are pressed together, totally violating the five-foot law. Does it make you feel anxious, defensive, or shut down? If a warrior can't create the space physically, he or she will create it at an energetic level by staying present with their experience. We can't always control external conditions, but we can control how we respond to them.

We discover as we work with our sense of boundaries most of the difficulties we face in our lives are directly or indirectly related to them. One of these difficulties involves the problem of victimization, which essentially grows out of the belief that we have no right to stand up for our own space. I feel so strongly about this very widespread issue that I've dedicated the next chapter to it. It is absolutely essential information for anyone choosing to pursue the warrior's path.

CHAPTER SIX

Owning Your Victim Self

*P*ART OF THE PROCESS of claiming our warrior is identifying the areas where we act like victims. The victim is someone who gives their power away. More accurately, it is someone who trades their power for something they want. Having lost their sense of power, they may end up feeling helpless, feeling hopeless, feeling they have limited choices or no choice at all.

Most of us act like victims at least some of the time. Your warrior's job is not to rescue your victim but to transform it, that is, to support you as you take your power back in those areas where you are feeling like a victim. To own our victim self we need to understand that there can be big payoffs for acting like a victim. You may get taken care of, you can blame others, nothing is ever your fault, and you don't have to take responsibility. You identify an adversary, polarize away from them, and never have to recognize that perhaps they embody qualities that you would rather deny in yourself. Our world is a mirror; whatever we refuse to own in ourselves we project on to the external world—which projects it right back at us. A victim refuses to see themselves in that mirror. Instead they see something or someone else. However, the price we pay for these projections is huge. Only in the areas in which we take responsibility for these projections can we change and reclaim our power. Only in the areas we own do we have any power. By refusing to own them we give our power away and become victims. A warrior knows there is no way to get through life without making mistakes, but only by owning them can we change them. I may create a mess in my life, but if I recognize it as my mess and accept that I created it, I can choose to change it or not.

In a larger context, I can look at my childhood and realize that terrible things were done to me when I was too little to do anything about them. But what I have come to know is that every experience was a teacher or a teaching that contributed to who I am. I believe that before we are born we write in our Book of Life everything we need to learn in this lifetime. I can look back and see what the lessons of my early life were about, what situations taught me courage, which ones taught me patience or honesty, and in the process find the blessing, the gold in the dross. For example, not having parents I could trust forced me at a very young age to seek the guidance and support of a higher authority. I looked to Divine Mother/Father for comfort and answers, which perhaps accelerated my spiritual journey in ways I might otherwise have never known. When I was in the midst of it, I was unable to see the teachings and felt like a victim, but now I can see how my Higher Self had a plan for me that was bigger than I understood at the time. Until I was able to recognize the process and trust it I felt like a victim. Until I was able to give up the "joys" of resentment, blame, self-pity and retribution, I was stuck in my victim role.

So how do we begin to identify where the victim lives in us? One way is to notice when we feel resentment. Resentment is anger that has been stuffed or disowned and allowed to fester. When it finally does get expressed it is often aimed at an inappropriate person or situation, grinding up an innocent bystander, a loved one, or even ourselves. A warrior expresses her anger in the present, in the moment that it is experienced. She expresses it in an appropriate way, takes responsibility for its expression, and releases it. A warrior is then willing to accept the consequences for her actions. This is clean, honest, direct behavior. A victim hides, holds, and cooks that anger and unloads it in ways that may not even be related to the original incident. It also eats away, internally, at the victim. I believe my mother's cancer was her anger turned to resentment and metastasized in her physical self. It literally devoured her. I had a terrible temper as a kid. I think I intuitively knew from watching her that if I didn't explode, I'd implode.

The other ways that we can identify where our victim is operating are when we blame others, feel helpless, make excuses, equivocate. Notice where you give it up. Where do you quit on yourself? Where do you feel you have no choice? Where do you feel that the problem is so big there's no way you can make a difference? The warrior is the part of us that *finds a way*, doing whatever it takes to get the job done.

While the warrior is governed by the second law of the Universe, Take Responsibility, the victim needs to Pay Attention (which is the first law of the Universe) to the third law of the Universe, No Kvetching. By applying this law we can begin to see where our victim operates. Begin now to listen to the voice of your victim:

> *"Can you believe what they did to me!"*
> *"It's not my fault."*
> *"Sorry I'm late, the traffic was awful."*
> *"It's your fault."*
> *"I can't afford it."*
> *"It's my parents' fault."*
> *"I don't have the time."*
> *"It was the bank's fault."*
> *"I hate my job."*
> *"It's the government's fault."*

"My wife (husband) doesn't understand me."
"It's God's fault."

When we are suffering from an illness, or we have a crime committed against us, our inner warrior will certainly let others know what's going on. However, the warrior's intent is to express what's going on so that he or she can find answers, make certain that perpetrators are caught, or recover what has been lost. And that's not kvetching. By contrast, victims see the crime or the health problem as just further evidence that the world is out to get them and therefore there's no point in attempting to be responsible for their own lives.

Acting like a victim is a habit like any other. To begin releasing ourselves from the victim habit we need to understand the steps for doing so. In the beginning the habit is unconscious behavior (the habit is doing you). Then you begin to notice the habit, and perhaps you watch it for a while. Maybe you become uncomfortable with it or it actually begins to cause you pain or you decide it no longer serves you. It's important to realize that in some way this habit has served you. It is a mechanism you set in motion in the past to keep you safe. For example, one of my habits has been *doing it all myself.* Because my emotional survival as a child was dependent on my not asking for anything, and our physical survival depended on my doing everything, this behavior became entrenched. As an adult it was difficult for me to ask for help, or accept it when it was offered. I often couldn't even hear the offer. I would find myself feeling exhausted, isolated, alienated, angry, and martyred. The *payoff* was independence; the *trade off* was in intimate relationships. Part of my warrior work has been learning to ask, and learning to accept, remembering that I'm not alone.

It's important to identify and honor the way in which your victim behavior once served you or it will resist change (which it will anyway, it's a matter of degree). You will bump up against your own resistance and denial, again and again.

Remember that the system is always perfect, you can trust your own process, and that you are always provided with whatever you need at any point to grow and change. And you are always made aware of when that point comes. You'll know when something that once may have saved you, no longer serves you. At the point when we make the decision to change we also need to choose what we want to do instead. Nature abhors a vacuum. If you empty out the psychic space, something else will quickly flow in to fill it. You can choose what that will be or leave it to chance.

Soon after we've made a decision to change we become acutely aware of our old habit, both in ourselves and others. We'll notice the habit after we've done it. At first this can be embarrassing or painful. Don't give yourself a hard time, just notice. Then you'll notice the habit when you're in the midst of it, and maybe you finish it anyway. Don't allow the voice of your judge or inner critic to overwhelm you; simply witness. You can say "I'm doing it again," and just pay attention, not "I'm doing it again, what a jerk I am." Stewart Wilde says, "Observation is power, judgment is weakness." Soon you'll notice the impulse to repeat the habit before it happens. This is a pivotal point because now you are doing the habit; it's no longer doing you. You can say yes or no to the habit at this point, rather than automatically falling into the old track. Soon you'll catch it before you do it , and choose not to. You'll repeat this for a while until one day you realize the habit is gone.

Take notice of each time you kvetch, blame, complain, make excuses, accuse, or resent and you'll soon see your life experience shift. You'll have more freedom in your life, more choices, more space, more time, and more fun as you shift from victim behavior to being someone who is in charge of your life. You'll also notice when other people in your life are acting their victim and be less willing to buy into it. It is not our job to change others, we can only change ourselves, which is how we change our world. But in refusing to collude with others when they assume victim roles, we can quietly be a mirror for them, if they are willing to see. The victim says we have no choice. The victim claims we have no power, which is simply not true. Warrior work is about choice and taking responsibility for our choices. It is by healing our inner victims that we reclaim our warrior self.

CHAPTER SEVEN

Facing Your Tyrants

*I*N THE PREVIOUS CHAPTERS, we introduced the first three laws of the Universe:

1. *Pay Attention:* Your life can't start until you show up.
2. *Take Responsibility:* What you don't own, owns you.
3. *No Kvetching:* Kvetching is the language of the victim.

The subject of tyrants brings us to the fourth law:

4. *Don't Take Any Shit.*

A tyrant is anything or anyone who tries to take your power away. Native Americans have an entire medicine wheel that teaches about tyrants. My friend Harley Swift Deer was very generous in sharing with me his knowledge of the Native American teachings about tyrants. Swift Deer is a teacher who knows how to play the tyrant himself for his students, and he has opened his heart and extensive knowledge to me in many ways.

If you can't recognize tyranny in its many forms, it will blindside you. There are internal and external tyrants, individual and collective tyrants, situational tyrants, and environmental tyrants, to name a few.

There are mental tyrants, such as critical parents, the boss that's never satisfied, anyone in authority that says they are better than you, the woman on the Virginia Slims® billboard who's looking down at your thighs. The worst tyrant of all however, is not any of these. Rather it is your own inner judge, banging his gavel in your brain, trying to convince you that you're "not enough," condemning you to a life of mediocrity. Most of us have a whole jury who sits up in our heads, commenting on everything we do: not good looking enough, not thin enough, not successful enough, rich enough, young enough, old enough, smart enough, talented enough, good enough. For anyone wishing to further explore how the inner critic limits our lives and how we can liberate ourselves from its tyranny, I highly recommend *Embracing Your Inner Critic: Turning Self Criticism Into a Creative Asset,* by Hal and Sidra Stone, published by Harper San Francisco.

Emotional tyrants could include the archetypal "Jewish mother" (of which I am one) or anyone who acts the martyr, manipulating through guilt and playing on our fear of disappointing them. Another emotional tyrant is the part of ourselves that refuses to forgive, that holds on to old wounds, actually nurturing the pain and expanding it. When I talk about forgiveness, I am not talking about letting a tyrant off the hook; only the tyrant can do that. Rather the process is one of releasing the hold a prior event, or person, has had on you through your own thought systems. When we look closely at old grievances, we quickly discover that the emotional pain we experience is ours and ours alone. We can choose to let it go or we can choose to go through the rest of our lives as prisoners of the past. In many cases our lack of forgiveness is closely linked with our need to control other people. Our anger toward a parent , for example, may be based on the fact that the parents we got aren't the ones we think we want. Forgiving your mother may be as simple as accepting the fact that she will never be like Donna Reed. Similarly, if we are to heal from the wound of early sexual abuse, we may have to let go of the need to have dad admit to what he did so that we can go on with healing whatever needs to be addressed in our own psyches.

Guilt is also an emotional tyrant. I happen to believe that it is the coin we use to pay for the possibility that we may want to do again what it is we feel guilty about. If you are finished with a behavior, and don't plan to repeat it, there is usually no guilt around it, only a feeling of satisfaction about overcoming a habit.

There is a saying that nobody can make us feel guilty, only we can do that. If this is true, we have to ask ourselves what the payoffs are. What are the benefits we derive from holding on to a thought system that limits our access to our warrior energy? Then we need to ask ourselves, is it worth it? One man, for example, was devastated almost weekly by phone calls from his parents who complained that he hadn't visited them in years. After looking at the guilt he realized that he experienced a peculiar sense of satisfaction with it. Exploring this further, he found that he looked upon his guilt as a sure sign that he had succeeded in punishing his parents. Once he'd seen this, he realized that all the reasons he wanted to punish them were from the past, and certainly not worth depriving himself of their companionship in the present. His next step was to pay them a surprise visit, which he did. They were delighted, and for the first time in his life this man allowed himself to take pleasure in their delight. Not long after this breakthrough, he realized how this guilt tyrant had limited his own warrior. He had carried over a similar pattern in all his close relationships, never allowing himself the luxury of enjoying other people's pleasure. This breakthrough not only revealed to him how he could free himself of his tyrants, it also opened the door to the power of shared pleasures in every area of his life, which is an important element in creating relationship and community. He quite literally opened up his heart center and supercharged that chakra.

A physical tyrant is the school yard bully. He is the steroid freak at the gym who pushes the space with his size. He is the higher ranking "belt" at a dojo who hurts his students. It's the guy who kicks sand in your face. It is also the part of yourself that has accidents, trips and falls, bangs your shin on the coffee table, slices your finger when you are chopping vegetables, smashes your thumb when you're driving a nail. The so-called accident-prone person is the one whose inner physical tyrants dole out far more punishment than any playground bully ever could. No one can work us over better than we can ourselves.

Sexual tyrants are sexual manipulators who use seduction for the purpose of controlling another, or commit rape in any of its many forms. A rapist is also a bully, rape being one of the most demoralizing and debilitating crimes one human can commit against another. It is right up there with murder because it can virtually kill the soul. Sexual harassment, sex in advertising, any system, individual or group which taught you to hate or fear your own body or your own sexuality are sexual tyrants. So is the part of yourself that says your breasts aren't big enough, your butt isn't tight enough or your penis isn't long enough. Also include high heels and push-up bras.

Spiritual tyrants include any person or system that tells you that you don't have your own direct connection to Source: the guru who gets you to give up your power and hand over your bankroll. It is the nuns who smacked my knuckles in Catechism class; the priest who told me I couldn't be an altar person because I was a girl. Anything is a tyrant that says God lives outside of us or we live outside of God.

The warrior sets boundaries with tyrants, draws a line, clearly states where the boundary is, and stands up for it. The warrior says to a tyrant, "You cannot act that way toward me." The woman whose husband constantly puts her down brings in her warrior self when she tells him, in no uncertain terms, that she will not put up with his negative remarks any more. Then she backs up her demands by putting him on notice that if he does it again, she's leaving—and follows through with this agreement the next time he does.

Once you have cleared the way for your warrior to act, he or she will back you up when you face your inner or outer tyrants and give you the courage to stand up to them. Your warrior will give you the integrity to speak your truth to them, the compassion not to judge them, and the wisdom to see them as part of yourself. Once we clear the tyrants out of our lives, it opens up our ability to see our higher purpose.

The parts of ourselves that we fear or refuse to own become our tyrants. They galvanize into action in time and space, manifest as real people or situations, so that we have to look at them. The religious right hates gays. It's obvious (to everyone but themselves) that what they really hate and fear is the part of themselves that is gay. We really are all androgynous beings and defining our ability to love by portals and protuberances is ridiculous. Some gays hate the religious right, who reflect the rigid, judgmental, pinchy asshole, critical part of themselves. They will continue to be tyrants for each other until each is willing to embrace the other side, or until they are both able to stop judging themselves. This is the evidence of one of the primary metaphysical principles: *You get what you have the consciousness for, one way or another.*

An example of a situational tyrant might be the hour and a half you spend in the doctor's office waiting for your appointment, or rush hour traffic, or the line at the bank. The warrior looks for choices. The victim kvetches. As a warrior, you can sit in the doctor's office and fill the time with something like reading, or meditating; as a victim you can make a scene and demand to be next, threaten to find another doctor, or simply leave. The victim in you will tell you to blast your horn to get things moving, get out and leave your car and take a bus; the warrior will counsel you to listen to music and plan your menu for the week. The victim might cut to the head of the line at the bank with the excuse that you have an emergency. The victim will fidget and get agitated, while your inner warrior will direct you to talk to the person next to you and perhaps meet a new friend.

Look for the pockets of chaos in your life and you'll nearly always find a tyrant. For me, time is a tyrant. I never seem to have enough of it. I act as if I don't really know how many hours there are in a day. But when I examine the issue clearly, step back and look, I realize it's not time but how I manage time that creates the chaos, so that makes me the tyrant. Let's see if that translates over to other areas in my life. Money is also a tyrant in my life. But once again, when I look objectively, it's not the money but how I manage the money that creates the chaos. Uh oh, there seems to be a theme here. Accountability, proper management of energy. This falls under the category of Take Responsibility, and probably, No Kvetching. Essentially, we can choose to give up our power to a tyrant, or we can keep it. Whatever you decide to do, recognize it as your choice. We will continue to find real people and come up against real situations to tyrannize us in our external reality until we recognize fully that they are only mirrors of what is going on in our internal selves.

We have environmental tyrants such as earthquake, flood, and fire. A victim will panic and become overwhelmed, giving up the ability to act. A warrior will stay present, in the moment, and be with the experience in a way which enables them to act appropriately and respond to the situation. If the Divine Mother is going to open up her giant maw and swallow you up, a warrior says, "Today is a good day to die. Let me at least experience my own death."

There are collective tyrants such as war, famine, plague. A victim is overwhelmed by the very magnitude of the problem and feels there is nothing they can do that could possibly make a difference. Tyrants deal with their fear by covering it up and trying to control the situation. A warrior knows you have to do what you can right where you are, and that is what makes the difference.

There are no glib or easy answers that apply to tyrants. However, paying attention is the place we start. If you want to release the warrior from the tyrants that are blocking its energies, pay close attention to those areas of your life where you feel most uncomfortable, and press into the resistance. Find the tyrant, identify it as clearly as you can. If it is an abusive spouse or boss, look at him or her squarely and openly. What is this person mirroring back to you in yourself? What's the part of you that actually draws you into the space where you are vulnerable to this person's tyranny? Where is the place in you that the tyrant hooks into, blocking you from your own power?

There are millions of people who stay in abusive relationships, or in jobs where their talents are never used, or in situations where they are misused by others or unable to express who they really are. However, the warrior in us always knows that the world is a big enough place to get anything we want from life—whether it's abuse or all the opportunities we need to embrace and fully actualize who we are.

Our tyrants can be our best teachers. They show us the parts of ourselves we have tried to exclude from our lives. They reveal to us where our work is. They give us the opportunity to practice our warrior skills.

Wherever you find a tyrant, you owe it to yourself to free yourself from its limitations. There are as many paths as there are people for this kind of growth and change. They can include meditation, working with a therapist or spiritual counselor, study and inner work, martial arts or any art form that focuses on its teaching as a spiritual discipline. Whatever path you choose, you now have the basic principles for charting your way out of the world of tyrants into the warrior's world.

CHAPTER EIGHT

Fear—
Piercing the Veil

HILE IT IS NOT ALWAYS easy to see it in the *busy-ness* of our everyday lives, our individual consciousness is a lens through which the light of Infinite Consciousness flows. As it flows through our lens, Divine Consciousness takes on the shape of our beliefs. Our beliefs are like filters, altering the shape of reality. There is *what is,* and then there is what we let ourselves see. Our filters act as a protective mechanism, limiting our reality according to what we can handle at any given time. In warrior work we are constantly pushing the envelope of awareness. In the Bible it says, "Now we look through the glass darkly, but then face to face . . . ," meaning that as we learn to see beyond the limits of our own lens we are rewarded by a clearer image of the truth, and a clearer understanding of *what is.* The warrior knows that it is only through this clear vision that we can meet the world head on and respond to our lives in an appropriate way.

One of the cloudiest filters we drop over the lens is fear. Fear is the veil that separates us from anything else, that keeps us from knowing our connection to everything else. An

important part of warrior work is learning how to take
responsibility for our fear and for the way our fear filters and
distorts reality. Some of these distortions can look like denial,
or anger, or attachment, or bigotry. When the context of our
lives is big enough, and we want to change the content, we
have to lift the filter. We lift the veil.

What do *you* think is on the other side of the veil?

What we go for in our workshops is to create the space for
our students to experience themselves, even if it is just for
one moment, with the veil lifted, to be in their reality without
the filters. When they do this, their lives are changed forever.

Out of our wounds our fear is born. We can't heal our fear
unless we are prepared to deal with the issues that created
that fear. Now, maybe I am afraid of heights, but you're not.
When we both stand on the edge of a cliff fear is a very palpa-
ble presence for me, but it doesn't exist there for you. What
that means is that its origin is within me. It is not some force
stalking the planet. Let's say we are walking in the woods and
a huge man steps into our path. The fear may paralyze you
while I simply check my moving center for intent. The way
for both of us to heal our individual fears is to identify their
source and then push the edge of that fear. For me that might
be remembering being held over an edge by a parent I didn't
trust. Then it might mean taking a ropes course with someone I do trust, so that I can renegotiate that fear in a safe way.
For you it might mean remembering sexual abuse from your
childhood. Then it might mean taking a good self-defense
course, one that prepares us to handle the emotional and psychological issues that inevitably come up when we face our
fears. They are what created the fear in the first place.

In our workshops, the difference between watching a student in the first round of combat—looking at the combat team
through their fear filter—and in the final round, when they
are standing in their present and looking clearly, is extraordinary. While they are looking through their fear filter, they see
what their fear projects and not what is really going on, so
they usually end up with their ass on the mat. When they use
their breath, and find their bellies they then have access to all

of the gifts of the moving center. They can read intent and get the first strike in, they have a sense of heightened awareness from using their adrenaline properly (improper breathing makes you dump your adrenaline). They have access to infinite resources, just like when the mom lifts the car off her kid. They have will, commitment, courage, they bring themselves fully into the present and engage with what is going on. Their warrior shows up.

I always remember Michael, who attended a workshop we gave in Florida. Like many men, he had never been in a real fight and didn't know if he was capable of defending himself in a street situation. He had a lot of fear about this because of the many stories in the news about street violence. He took the workshop specifically to test himself and to learn about his own inner warrior. Three months after his training, he was jogging in an unfamiliar neighborhood when four young men started harrassing him. They wanted his money and his expensive running shoes. Michael told me, "You taught me that once you know you're going to be attacked, you take the initiative. So I attacked the closest one to me. First I kicked him in the groin, and when he bent over I kicked him in the head and shoved him into a pile of trash. The other three were standing there with their mouths open, and then they just took off running. At first, I was shaking like a leaf, and then I thought, 'Wow! I just fought off four guys!'"

Your warrior's job is to deal with your fear. The appropriate purpose for fear, as we have discussed, is as part of your internal warning system. It lives in your belly, where your warrior lives. It's one of the tools the warrior uses to keep you safe.

One of the first techniques we teach our students is the use of the breath, how to breath themselves past the paralysis of fear and into their bellies so that they can act; respond appropriately to danger, or just respond to life. Most people disassociate when in fear, which takes you out of the present and puts you at fear's mercy. You can't deal with something if you're not there. We disassociate when we are afraid something terrible is going to happen and we don't want to be there when it does. It is a survival mechanism that got set up when we were little and bad things happened to us that we couldn't do anything about. Your warrior shows up in your present to keep you safe from danger and face your tyrants. You trust your warrior to never abandon you, so you no longer have to abandon yourself. The use of the warrior breath brings us into the present, which is where we face our fears. It is usually the anticipation of the thing feared that defeats us. Time after time we have students report back to us about overcoming what looked like insurmountable tasks, handling situations they had avoided out of fear all their lives, or protecting themselves against physical assault, that by simply staying in their bellies with their breath the thing feared was easily overcome. Fear is our biggest tyrant, treat it like any other tyrant. Set your boundaries, stand up for them, be willing to do whatever it takes to take your power back.

The warrior knows that fear is the edge between the known and the unknown. In order to go on our adventures, fall in love, find our dreams, or even break our habits, we have to step over the edge.

*T*YRANTS OF OUR TIME

We live in interesting times. The ancient Chinese viewed interesting times as a curse. But I prefer to see our era as an opportunity. We have so many choices, an incredible palette of experience available to us. There is a lot of fear-mongering going on right now. We have forecast our doom in everything from ETs to pole shifts, to geological disasters, to nuclear holocaust, to the Antichrist. Between psychic predictions and the Revelations, it doesn't look too good. It is infinitely fascinating and mesmerizing to get caught up in this drama, and it is true that each of us has come through with a role to play, a job to do. But remember what is real, that consciousness creates, and that we are cocreators with God.

What do you think God desires for us? And what do we desire for ourselves? It's time to get those two agendas in alignment.

How can we begin to find that alignment? One way is, break down the walls. Remember, it's your warrior's job to set boundaries, and if you know how to set boundaries, you don't need walls.

So reach out to everyone, to everything, and then notice when fear stops you. Speak to that stranger, look him in the eye, and make contact instead of looking away, pretending you're too busy, or too important, or not important enough, or that you don't care or care too much, to include him in your life. Reach out, and see what stops you. "They'll think I'm weird," "*They won't think I'm cool,*" "They might reject me." Notice what form your fear takes. Then, Do It Anyway, which is The fifth law of the Universe in the warrior's code. No risk, no reward.

We fear what we are separate from. The way a master martial artist works is this: he doesn't identify anyone as an adversary. He knows we are all part of the same Self. So, you cannot have a thought or make a move that is not also his own. Within this way of perceiving the world, it becomes not a question of defeating but of embracing one's "apparent" opponent, all the while recognizing that we have no opponents outside ourselves.

Daniel was able to sit with the lions in their den because he knew the lion in himself. If he had not, his fear would have gotten him eaten.

The things that we can use to "take ourselves out" are the same things that we can use to wake ourselves up. That includes our fear.

Every time we fearlessly, or in spite of our fear, open our hearts just a little more to the people in our lives, we create family. Every time we open our circle to include another, we have extended our family and created community. So we meet the resistance, and We Do It Anyway, and pretty soon we realize that what we have done is create a better world because we have been willing to overcome our fears.

I'm not trying to say that the task before us isn't huge, because it is. That task requires us to renegotiate our relationship to fear. What I'm here to tell you is that we are equal to the job. We are never asked to do more than we can handle, or less. The Universe doesn't set us up for failure.

How do I know? Because time after time, I have seen our students, ordinary humans—secretaries, construction workers, college students, attorneys, housewives, therapists, teenagers, elders, athletes, people in wheelchairs—I have seen them confront their fears and overcome them. I have seen them believe in themselves and create miracles, and realize that what we have come to view as miracles are nothing more than looking at ourselves, each other, and our world without the filter of fear. Not through a glass darkly, but face to face with God.

CHAPTER NINE

Lightening Up

*T*HE WARRIOR'S PATH is not all hard work and rigorous discipline. Coming into our own power also includes play and fun. This chapter is to remind us that the warrior spirit is energized by our ability to fill out our life experience through revitalizing our relationship with the natural world. It is the wild mind, the ability to enjoy the unexpected, to reconnect with the child's heart within us, to play with the animals and become beginners in life once again that restores the soul and recharges our energy, making us whole again. Warrior work is about returning to our natural selves, our innocence, our true selves. It is so easy, particularly when we are just beginning the warrior's path, to forget to keep a balance between work and play, between the civilized and the wild minds in ourselves. The journey home doesn't have to be a forced march, it should be a dance. To these ends I offer the following prescriptions, which should be taken in daily doses.

Spend some time in nature, plant a garden, take your dog to the beach. If you don't have a dog, get one. Or a cat (don't take your cat to the beach).

Tell someone besides your therapist your story, the real story. Ask someone to share their story. And really listen. Talk to the animals, listen, really listen to them.

Our Golden Retriever, Shilo (also known as Pooh Bear, Pookey Face, or Honey Boy), was a gift to us from two of our friends. For the first two years we thought maybe they gave us the dog because they were mad at us. He was a one dog demolition derby. But he has somehow been magically transformed into a great dog. He is our resident heyoka*; he never lets us work too long or take ourselves too seriously. If I'm at my desk after 5 P.M., he starts nudging me and dropping toys in my lap. He gives me a warning at about 4:30, putting his head in my lap and giving me a soulful look with his big brown eyes, letting me know I'd better start winding it up. Serious nudging starts at 5 P.M.

The last time we packed to travel for a workshop, Shilo dropped a few of his toys in the suitcase. Just a reminder to walk our talk while we were gone.

Our cat Mocha (otherwise known as Chu Chu or Cut That Out You Little Devil!) likes to play Kung Fu. He will wait around a corner for me and leap out unexpectedly, attaching himself to my leg. Sometimes he'll stalk me, circling and batting at me with his paws, claws covered (usually). I watch him when we let him out in the morning: stretching languidly, then sitting and surveying his domain for a moment, deciding what adventure to embark on today.

He is the wildest of our animals and I love his feral nature and the way he speaks to that same nature in me. We could all take lessons from him, stepping out into our world every morning, taking a moment to take in its beauty, and deciding what adventure we shall pursue today.

Anyone who is a pleaser should get a cat. Cats flat don't give a damn what you think. They know they don't need to earn your love, that it's your privilege to love them. Cats don't equivocate.

---

* In the Native American tradition a Heyoka is a sacred clown.

Miss Mouse, our other cat, is very petite and feminine, slightly cross-eyed, white with apricot ears and tail. Having spent the first part of her life under a truck in a junk yard eating lizards, she has developed her creature comforts to a fine art. She always finds the softest, sunniest spots to snooze in. Lying on the heater vent is a particular favorite. She refuses commercial cat food, insisting on fresh fish, beef or turkey, which I have to cook for her. I tried to explain to her that I am a vegetarian and don't exactly relish this job. She just looks at me in her steady, blue eyed, cross-eyed way, and waits to be served. She will reward me for my efforts by standing up on her hind legs with her paws straight up in the air, to let me know I may pick her up and cuddle her.

Mocha was a gift to us from his mother. Bob and I were driving down a busy street in Los Angeles one day when we saw a mama cat carrying a kitten in her mouth. We stopped and tried to find out where she lived and were told she was a stray. I tried to catch her, but she wouldn't let me. So I sat down near her and got quiet. She stared at me for a while, then picked up her kitten, put him down in front of me, walked away, sat back down and stared at me. How could I refuse!

We also have a little lovebird, Noah (affectionately known as Squirty or Little Beak). This little morsel of life packs a lot of mischief, love, and spirit in a couple of ounces. Only Divine Mind could come up with such a great design. He is the fiercest of all our animals, a little warrior bird. He has been known to lure Mocha the Cat over to his cage with a kernel of corn in his beak (our cat loves corn) and bite him on the nose when he gets close enough. Noah was also a gift from two of our friends, given to us as a fledgling. It's an incredible feeling to have something willingly fly to you.

Mr. and Mrs. Fish live in their ten-gallon ecosystem in my kitchen. They are a constant reminder to me of our planet's delicate balance. They recently gave me a teaching on abundance. Watching them I suddenly realized that I'm sitting in a fishbowl in the middle of the ocean, surrounded by a world of unlimited possibility. If I'm feeling limited by the tank, all I have to do is swim out the top.

Animals offer us unconditional love; they carry our shadow, take on our anger and violence, don't judge us, offer themselves up as companions, food, fodder, whatever we ask. They never forget their connection to *The All That Is* and are always there to help us remember ours. They know when to resist, when to fight, and when to surrender. Above all, they know how to play.

> And we consider animals a lesser species than us.
> Hah! We are,
> Blind as bats
> Stubborn as mules
> Dumb as oxen
> Crazy as loons

If the fifth law of the Universe, which we discussed in Chapter Eight is, *So What, Do It Anyway,* the sixth Law is, *Keep Your Sense of Humor.* The nice thing about these laws is you can rearrange their order according to what's going on in your life. You can toss them out, or ignore them completely. Laughter is cosmic glue. It is a way of appreciating, of enjoying, of including something in your experience. It can bring us together in a way that nothing else can. The more we include laughter in our lives the simpler our lives get.

Become a people watcher. Sit in a park, or stand on the street and notice people, really notice. Find one thing about each individual that is beautiful. Let yourself take this beauty in. Maybe that guy over there has kind eyes; notice them, appreciate their beauty. Then find one silly thing. Maybe that same guy is wearing a tie. Can't get much sillier than that. Ties are the karma guys get (we've got them by the throat) for talking women into wearing high heels, a contemporary form of hobbling (we pretend we can't run away).

Look in the mirror and find something beautiful about yourself. Find something silly, and appreciate both.

A spiritual teacher of mine once said, "Remember, you're the silliest thing you've got."

Look for the absurd and let yourself laugh at it. Watch the *soaps,* read *People* magazine. Watch another ridiculous movie where the heroine has to be rescued by the hero. Look for the caricatures and stereotypes, like the *Sports Illustrated* swimsuit issue.

Look in the mirrors that don't lie. One way to do this is make friends with a child. When my young friend Heather was five years old, she nicknamed me Silly Cat Face, a name that is entirely appropriate for the times I'm taking myself too seriously.

Because many of us come from dysfunctional families and were abused one way or another, we are afraid of children because they remind us of our pain. Like our animals, they also see us for who we are. Unlike our animals, they might tell, which makes them doubly dangerous—and doubly valuable in terms of our growth.

As we allow our own inner children room in our lives to play, knowing that our warrior is there to keep them safe, we begin to create more room in our world for all the little ones, the keepers of our innocence, our trust and our joy.

Henry Miller said, "The thing is, to become a Master and in your old age to acquire the courage to do what children did before they knew anything."

We human beings were not designed to live as most of us live, spending eight to ten hours a day in survival mode, living in our little pods, sealed away from each other, giving the care and education of our children over to strangers, abandoning our parents to strangers and letting them die alone and away from home. Almost everyone I know is at least a little bit lonely, exhausted, and stressed out. Imagine a world where we live in extended families, sharing our chores, our children, our resources, sitting together and listening to each other's stories, caring for our grandparents, sitting with the elders and honoring their wisdom, sharing our gifts, asking for what we want, accepting what we need, giving freely of what we have, resolving our conflicts as a community, sitting in counsel with ourselves, our elders, and our children, where everyone has a voice. What if we danced together, dreamed together, sang together, talked together, drummed together, planned together, played together. What if we freed ourselves of the belief that there isn't enough time, money, resources, love. What if we all swam out of the top of the tank.

The task at hand is simple: to change the things that are no longer working for us, first in ourselves and then in our world. A better world begins with each of us. Simple, not easy. But possible. And necessary,

Although there is great satisfaction in the work itself, warrior work can be tough, requiring discipline, perseverance, patience, commitment, accountability, and sometimes sacrifice. It's important to keep in mind what we are working for. The spirit of play is not only one of the ways to get there, but part of the destination itself.

My friend Phyllis once said to me, "What if I were to tell you that you have been given a huge inheritance, and all you have to do is claim it?" That inheritance is joy.

Each year, in my own life and in the life of the many students who come through the workshop, I am more and more convinced that joy is everyone's inheritance. The sad thing is that we've forgotten how to claim it. Perhaps the suggestions in this chapter will help us accept what is ours.

CHAPTER TEN

Gratitude and Grace

*G*RATITUDE IS THE ABILITY to accept God's gifts. Everything we need is always there. It is our gratitude that allows it into our experience. I think of my mother as one of my greatest teachers in this. I wouldn't be teaching warrior skills today if she hadn't been a tough adversary. So the challenges the Universe provided through her turned out to be a gift. But it wasn't until I understood that some of our most important lessons come from our toughest challenges that I was able to teach warrior skills. Taking that realization in was a lesson in gratitude. And then when I finally realized I could choose another way to learn, that was a lesson in grace.

Without gratitude, nothing has any value. We never learn to appreciate or use the gifts provided us. Without grace, we never learn to trust our partnership with God. Without gratitude and grace, the warrior cannot accept or use the experiences that come into his or her life.

Gratitude is not taking anything for granted.

When my dear friend Randy Love was in intensive care with Guilliame Barre disease, a very rare and potentially deadly virus, I looked at him, tied down, lying unconscious, every orifice in his body stuffed with some tube, and I was reminded not to take love for granted. When we learned he was going to be all right, I was overwhelmed with gratitude and I thought, "If at any moment I forget to appreciate you, experience you, be present with you, let me remember how it felt when we almost lost you."

I was also grateful for the Western technology that saved him even as I was angry at what they wouldn't allow as part of his healing process. They isolated him from all but a few of us, even trying to keep his wife, Liz, from his side. The nurse who told her she couldn't be with him didn't know what she was up against. Liz is a force to be reckoned with. Big Nurse is lucky she didn't find herself trussed up with catheter tubing and stuffed in a utility closet.

I wanted us all to sit with him, pray for him, surround him with our love. Chris, who is part of my support team and who held me while I wailed my outrage at the possibility that Randy might leave us, reminded me that he would hear our prayers from a distance. She reminded me that the extra physical distance just forces us to be better alchemists.

When things are going great, gratitude is easy, although even then we often forget. Gratitude when things are tough is not so easy, but it can provide the energy to turn things around.

So your wife left you, you lost your job, they're repossessing your house, your dog died, and you just found out that you have cancer. Be grateful that you are a powerful enough being to create conditions of such magnitude. When you are ready, you have the power to change them, to learn from them, or to accept with grace lessons whose purpose you cannot yet even imagine. I believe that even in crisis and hardship, if we look behind what appears to be adversity, we'll see God's plan, part of which is getting us over ourselves and our egos.

Gratitude and grace are inner qualities, the qualities of a spiritual warrior. The key ingredient they both share is surrender. To a soldier surrender means giving up or giving in to a force outside of himself. Depletion. A warrior knows surrender means becoming part of a power bigger than himself. Completion. Gratitude and grace are both warrior skills that enable us to deal with difficult times, to handle adversity, to look beyond the material to the spiritual picture and to trust ourselves and our universe. Together, gratitude and grace allow us to feel, from deep within us, how the blessings of our lives elevate us and give us strength.

We can all use a little practice in expressing gratitude, so here's a simple exercise: when you use a paper towel, thank the tree. Have some toast, thank the wheat. Scramble an egg, thank the chicken. Sauté some vegetables, thank Grandmother Earth. Do this for a while and it will start to bring things into sharper focus and you'll begin to notice how much more you value what you have in your life.

Writing this book has greatly expanded my sense of gratitude. The writing prompted me to look at my world and I realized how many of my dreams have already come true. Since I started writing I have become more aware, on a daily basis, of all of my blessings.

Gratitude allows us to experience grace.

Grace is the law of allowing. It usually comes after that moment of letting go. William Butler Yeats spoke of that moment when after much practice and discipline, all your efforts come together and you "Cannot tell the dancer from the dance."

Where it usually breaks down for me is the point at which I say, "OK God, great job so far, I'll take it from here," that's right before the moment of surrender. But instead of surrendering and taking in all that God offers, I slip back into my "I can handle it all myself" mode.

And once again, I find myself pinned to the mat.

Without grace the samurai loses his life, or at least a limb; the modern day spiritual warrior falls back into the old, limiting beliefs and perceptions that made him or her a victim.

One of the first things we teach our students is, don't struggle, don't go force against force, or resist force. Follow the flow of energy in and you'll find your target area, or goal.

The truth is, I love a good fight. If you pay attention, and follow the rest of the ten laws in the warrior's code, a good fight will almost always lead you right into your power. I'm not, of course, talking about going out and picking fights, or inventing them. Normal life provides enough of them, whether it's a fight with the phone company about an over-charge or a fight with a neighbor over a barking dog. How-ever, when we approach such conflicts with our mind attuned to the warrior's code, we invariably end up learning from them rather than getting locked into a situation where there can only be one winner and one loser.

At those times that I don't abide by the warrior's code, my love of a good fight invariably takes me right into pain and struggle. Sometimes, the pain and struggle that results includes the loss not only of gratitude and grace but simple dignity as well—like the time I arm wrestled with a sponsor at a popular restaurant in Grand Rapids, Michigan.

I kept looking for a worthy adversary, creating bigger and bigger opponents, testing my chops, pushing the edge. Know-ing my love of a good battle, my daughter used to aim me and fire me like a canon at anyone she perceived as a threat. And I did her bidding like the good soldier I was in those days.

My Uncle George was an early model for me in this kind of combative behavior. We listened to his stories about taking on the IRS and the unions, and winning. We listened to stories about Aunt Mary riding shotgun—literally with a shotgun—getting the cash receipts to the bank. On his 79th birthday Uncle George celebrated by decking some guy who crashed his party. He passed away November 2, 1998. And at 89 he still liked a good fight.

Somewhere along the line, I realized that because of the way I grew up, I identified my life with struggle. One of the ways I invested value in something was by how hard I had to fight to get it. When I was younger, everything had a price and that price was usually pain. I've had to learn to turn what began as a survival mechanism, and became a destructive system, into a productive process, so that I could take myself through the teachings without taking myself out. It was, I suppose, a transformation from grit to grace.

Gratitude and grace are solid warrior skills, whether we are talking to God, or talking to some guy in an alley who's threatening us with a knife. A warrior knows she must first turn inward before she can turn outward. She must turn it over (gratitude) before she can turn it around. We have to let it go (grace) before we can let it in.

It all comes down to learning a new way to say thank you for everything that comes into our lives, and then find the lessons that free us to open up to all that we are.

⁊lONATTACHMENT AND THE POWER OF GRACE

Included in the principle of grace is the concept of nonattachment. Grace comes from letting go. Many religious systems teach that this means you should give it up to them. You give them your money, your power, your own authority. We hand it all over to a guru, a pope, a preacher because *they* are enlightened enough not to get caught in it and *we're* not. What the warrior knows is that we set our own snares and get caught in them so that we can learn how to free ourselves. A warrior trusts his own truth and his own direct connection to Source. A warrior knows that all learning unfolds from within and all a teacher ever does is precipitate awareness. A warrior knows that nonattachment is the understanding that everything is a manifestation of consciousness so we can always re-create the material picture. The warrior trusts the Universe to provide him with everything he needs, right at that moment of need, and that his job is simply to look for what God is saying to him through his own experience. A warrior honors everything as a teacher or a teaching. That is gratitude and grace.

I kept looking for bigger and bigger adversaries in my life, until I found myself in the ring, squared off with God. And the voice inside me said, "Why do you resist Me?" In that moment I gave it all up, and remembered where it all came from.

TRY THIS

Take some time every day to count your blessings, the obvious and not so obvious ones. Start a list of things you are grateful for and add to it every day. Include the people, the animals, the places, the events, your work, your possessions, music, art, the flowers, the trees; whatever you have in your experience that contributes to your life. Look, *really look,* around you. After a week, begin to look at all of the things in your life you have considered adversity. Take one thing a day, and look for the teaching, the blessing in it. Sit with it until you find at least one thing, no matter how small, about this adverse experience that contributed to your life.

Focus for a moment on a person or situation in your life that makes you feel fearful, angry, resentful, or righteously indignant. Say to yourself or the Universe, "Thank you for this teaching. But could you offer it to me in a gentler form, one that I can more easily take in?" Then imagine how the lesson might be taught by a teacher who loves you dearly and who will patiently work with you until you've got the lesson at last. Imagine them being with you as you face the difficult person or situation. Turn to him or her for guidance every time you feel challenged. Thank them each time for their love and support.

CHAPTER ELEVEN

Agreements

A WARRIOR IS ONLY as good as his word.

Being as good as our word is the way we build trust in ourselves. And it is the way we earn the trust of others.

The importance of trust becomes clear when we stop to realize that if we can't depend on the warrior to *show up* when she's agreed to show up, it doesn't matter how strong, skillful, or intelligent she is, she won't be much of an asset to our cause. Similarly, if we're to build self-esteem and self-trust, we have to know that when we make an agreement, we're going to put everything we are behind it. Through our ability to make and keep our agreements, we focus our intent, and without this focus, we collapse in upon ourselves.

My Uncle George promised his father he would see to it the grandchildren were taken care of. When my mother and her sister tried to take the college funds our grandfather had left us, Uncle George stepped in and stopped them, even though he knew it would cost him his relationship with his sisters. If he gave you his word, you could take it to the bank. I promised my brother and sister I would take care of them even though it cost me my freedom. My uncle was my model for keeping my word. He taught me that the cost for breaking my agreement would have been my integrity, a price I would have paid for the rest of my life. As it turns out, I lost nothing by keeping my word to my siblings. I gained everything. I learned that we build trust in ourselves and discover the meaning of personal integrity through the way we handle our agreements. And it is through making agreements and keeping them that we earn the trust of others.

Webster's defines integrity as firm adherence to a code of moral values, incorruptibility, a state of being undivided. Of being whole. Warrior work is about claiming our wholeness and we do that by being in our integrity. One of the most important ways we accomplish this is by keeping our agreements.

Earlier we explored the role of boundaries in the warrior's life. In the process of setting boundaries, agreements are key. Boundary setting begins and ends with agreements, first with yourself, defining your safe space, then with others, naming that space and asking that it be honored. If someone crosses that boundary without your consent, the agreement is violated and it breaks trust in them. If you don't stand up for your boundary and it gets crossed, you break trust with yourself. It's important to understand that agreements can be renegotiated but while they are in effect they need to be honored.

The warrior skills we bring to making agreements are those of integrity, speaking our truth, the honesty to ask for what we need, the courage to stand up for what we believe, not letting ourselves or others off the hook, and demanding accountability from ourselves and others.

There is an exercise that we do in our workshop called the "Warrior Task." It is about agreements. The Warrior Task reveals to our students where they *stand up* and where they *give up*. Through it they get to see very clearly what stops them (if anything does) from keeping their agreements with themselves and others. What they experience in this task becomes a metaphor teaching them where they give up their power in their lives. It shows them where their edge is and what stops them from pushing that edge. Part of the exercise reveals where they give up on themselves; the other part reveals where they give up on others. The message is a simple one: *We cannot afford to watch another train to Auschwitz pass and pretend we don't know where it's going.*

For some, what stops them is the fear of asking another person to be there for them; for others it's the fear of having to be there for someone else. For some, it's speaking the truth; for others, it's hearing the truth. For all of us, it's about what we are willing to risk. It takes courage to give up our illusions, in order to seek out and commit ourselves to our personal vision, the inner truth which gives our life its purpose and meaning. When we make an agreement with ourselves to commit to that path, we discover what it truly means to focus our intent. It's about whether or not we are willing to put our ass on the line to create the world we want. It's one of the greatest ironies that we spend so much of our energy avoiding the job we were put here to do, the gift we were given to share with the world and through which we can experience our greatest fulfillment. This must be what k.d. lang and Ben Mivik were reflecting on in their song, "Save Me," where they say, "Save me from you/ But pave me/ The way to you."

Joseph Campbell called it "following your bliss," and spoke of what a paradox it was that most of us would do anything to avoid committing ourselves to that path.

One of the things our students get to look at when they do their warrior's task is all of the excuses they make for not keeping their agreements. Excuses give us a lot of control, but at the expense of sacrificing our power.

During one workshop, a woman who had been making excuses all her life recognized the consequences, the price she was paying for this habit. She said, "The real message I'm giving myself every time I make an excuse is that I'm helpless to do anything about my life!" She had hit on the core of the role of keeping our agreements, that excuses for not keeping them keep us victims.

The excuses people use for not taking the workshop are often the same things that keep them from getting what they want in their lives:

"I can't afford it."
"I don't have the time."
"I have the kids that weekend."
"I'm too out of shape."
"My husband (wife) won't let me."

Every excuse usually turns out to be just another way of saying "I'm scared."

And most of the fear we experience is based on past agreements which were either badly negotiated or out and out violated. Let's explore that a little. Most of us haven't had very good models for making and keeping agreements. Perhaps a parent broke trust with you early on by making promises that were seldom kept; or perhaps you modeled your behavior after a parent who was always making excuses. Most families have hidden agendas—conflicting agreements that run at the same time—either consciously or unconsciously.

For example, when a parent refuses to see us as who we really are, because it doesn't fit their agenda, that's a broken agreement. In the ideal world parents have a responsibility to discover who we truly are, and nurture our inherent gifts. It also demands of a child that they break a primary agreement with themselves—that they be true to themselves. A writer friend recently told me about just such a double message, one that would make a great comic routine for Jackie Mason. My friend's mother always said, "I just want my son to be happy and successful, just be whatever he wants to be—a doctor, a lawyer, it doesn't matter!" Somehow my friend slipped through the net and became a writer, which was what made him happy.

We have a graduate of the warrior work, the younger of two brothers, who at two was stolen by his father from his mother. His father tacitly asked him to agree not to love his mother, to forget her. As a small child his survival required that he comply. But there was a deeper truth that caused him feelings of conflict. His heart required that he refuse, though he pretended to hold that agreement for many years. He was also silently asked to agree not to be as good as his older brother, at anything. His survival required him to comply to these agreements that were pressed on him. In spite of the fact that they were supposed to be a lifetime contract, there came a point when he had to look at the truth. First, his creativity, no longer agreeing to be suppressed, emerged in a way that made it impossible for him to deny himself any longer. In the beginning, the emergence of this truth disrupted his entire life. Letting go of the old agreements, even knowing they were false, caused him great confusion and fear. A powerful voice within him said, "I never agreed to make that deal, and now you have to deal with me." He began to listen to that voice, recognizing that it represented his own truth. Since then he has turned his life around, honoring his own gifts and going for his own dreams. He also has faced his family and said, "I won't agree to be in your shadow anymore." He freed himself to follow his own creativity, his own dreams, and the right to choose who and how he loves, including the right to reconnect with his mother, which he did. This is truly an example of a person finding the warrior path and discovering his own power.

The good news is when something is no longer working for you, you get to renegotiate the agreement. That might involve agreements you made with your parents, or with a spouse; the "don't rock the boat" agreements. To move on and to grow, these agreements need be renegotiated. We need to be able to say to each other, "This is no longer working for me. Things need to change."

Take a look at the areas in your life where you break your agreements. Look closely at the times you are late (some people who are habitually late use it as an act of petty tyranny, a way to manipulate others). Maybe you bounced a check. And what about the call you didn't return? There's the diet you didn't stay on (don't make promises you can't keep), and all those unkept New Year's resolutions. How do you feel when you think about a broken agreement? (Check your gut.) How do you feel when you think about agreements you have kept? In which case do you feel weakened or victimized? And in which case do you feel empowered?

It's the little transgressions, just like the little acts of heroism, that make up the quality of our lives.

Look for all the unspoken agreements in your life. For example:

> *"I won't tell if you won't tell."*
>
> *"I won't call you on your stuff if you won't call me on mine."*

Look very closely at these and ask yourself what price you are paying for them, and what your life might look like if you renegotiated them to reflect your truth today.

Everything in our life is based on agreements, either conscious or unconscious. So there is not a single person for whom this isn't relevant. Just as action has consequences, so does inaction. Not voting is agreeing to live by someone else's rules. And this is true even when there is nothing on the ballot that you feel deserves your vote.

When we turn our face away, when we keep quiet in the presence of injustice, when we don't stand up to tyranny, all these are an agreement to live by someone else's rules.

Where have we agreed to sacrifice someone else's well-being or reputation in order to save face, or save our own ass? These are agreements to live out of integrity.

There are some huge collective false agreements operating in our society, collusions in which each one of us takes a part, even if it's only a minor one. Every collusion reduces our power. When we collude with institutions or individuals, we give our power away.

Racism, genderism, ageism, lies by the tobacco companies, economic exploitation by the AMA, graft and lack of integrity in our educational, political, religious, and military systems—all these agreements are designed to disempower. A warrior refuses to collude. A warrior knows what it means to come out, to stand in one's own power and be separate. What we are up to is nothing less than redefining our world on our own terms.

Did you think the warrior's path would be easy? It's far more than a few more minutes of meditation, or sending off a few more dollars to Greenpeace. As warriors we are going to have to bring everything we are to the table.

I spent a long time doing work that I believed in, teaching the Warrior Within workshops, working to the point of exhaustion, not making any money, the only measurable success being in seeing how the work changed our students' lives. I knew I had a message to deliver. I knew that I had made an agreement with the Universe to do this work, but for so many years it was a struggle. The work was incredibly satisfying. But as everyone knows, satisfaction alone doesn't pay the rent. There were times when I nearly gave into despair. I'd check inside and ask, "What would you have me do?" and I always got the same answer, "Don't Quit."

The poet Rainer Maria Rilke says, when you don't have the answers, live the questions. And so we did.

Bob and I went through some incredible hardships, not abandoning what we believed to be our mission. It was a dark night of the soul. One of the blessings was that we had each other's companionship and support going through it. At a point at which we really felt we had hit the wall, the message came. We knew this planet was going to see some very tough times, and we were just asked to go first so that we could help build a bridge to the other side. And on some level we had agreed to do that.

So we lived the question, trusting ourselves, and the Universe.

I know that many of you have suffered losses of jobs, money, security, loved ones. Through all of it, there's one agreement to always keep with yourself, *Don't Quit.* Remember, you can never lose what's real. And whatever is left standing will be enough. *Don't Quit,* the seventh law of the Universe, is the bottom line agreement that never needs to be renegotiated.

In today's world it isn't easy to follow the seventh law. All the old systems are breaking down. Political systems, educational systems, religious systems are all experiencing upheaval and turmoil. In the midst of it, it becomes increasingly difficult to maintain agreements or decide which ones to renegotiate. The earth herself is changing, with increased incidence of earthquake, flood, fire, and hostile weather. In the Hindu tradition, Kali Ma does her dance at the end of the world, trampling everything, and out of the rubble a new world is born. We can only assume that this is what's going on, in which case our skills as spiritual warriors are going to be greatly needed for our survival.

Even though the old systems aren't working anymore, they will fight for their life, the same way old habits fight when we try to change them. And the same way our old defenses will fight for control when they sense we are ready to let the Higher Self step in. You can be sure that when these old systems sense that they are losing the battle their tactics get increasingly aggressive, and when that doesn't work, increasingly subtle, which is why we have to Pay Attention.

We are changing the old agreements. We are taking our warrior with us to the bargaining table and we are renegotiating the deal.

I know it looks like chaos, but it's really evolution.

Awhile back I had a dream. I was tending the altar of a Goddess. On her altar was a beautiful life-sized statue of Her. As I was placing flowers on the altar, She came to life and said to me, "If you surrender to Me, I will enter you." I became very afraid. I thought I would lose my identity. I resisted Her. She said, "It is your choice." So, with much trepidation, I agreed. I closed my eyes and merged with Her. I instantly found myself traveling through my world at an incredible speed. I was traveling so fast, everything else seemed to be standing still. In front of me was a steering wheel, and for a moment I became fearful that unless I grabbed the wheel we would collide with the other objects we were nearly missing while zooming past. I heard the voice of the Goddess inside me say, "If you put your hands on the wheel, you'll crash."

So I sat back and enjoyed the ride.

The dream made it clear to me that there is a Higher Power in charge of this journey our entire planet is on at this time. Our agreement must be that we will not presume to know more than She and start wrestling with the wheel.

If you start to doubt yourself, breathe yourself into your belly, where your warrior lives, where there is no self-doubt. And if you start to lose faith, remember, it is against God's nature to let you down. Divine Mind has agreed to eternally care for Its Idea. Anytime we feel let down it is not by God but by our own illusions—when we grab the wheel and try to wrestle the Universe out of God's control.

In your Book of Life, you wrote down the teachings that you needed to get and the experiences you wanted to have in this chapter in your life. You may not remember why you wanted these lessons but you agreed to take them on and now no one can do them but you.

There is an underlying agreement that the warrior in each of us knows. In our quiet moments we feel its presence.

We cut a deal with God.

We are spiritual beings who wanted to experience physical form, to know what it was like to inhabit a body, experience our feelings, our emotions, our sexuality. We wanted to taste, touch, feel, hear, see, and smell. We wanted wind in our hair, grass under our feet; we wanted to make love, eat pasta, drink wine, stroke a cat, play the piano, smell the jasmine, listen to Bach, ride a Harley, nurse an infant, see a sunset, write a book. . . .

We wanted to have an adventure, so we agreed to forget that we ourselves are the adventure. We agreed to separate from God so that we could make the journey home, and experience the joy of reunion.

Each lesson we learn through making agreements, keeping our agreements, renegotiating agreements to honor who we really are, and even the agreements we break, takes us further along on our journey. Our power is increased in direct proportion to our awareness of this process and how it affects our lives.

A very good friend of mine, Peter, (the name is changed to protect the guilty) was habitually late. I found myself waiting a minimum of twenty minutes to half an hour for Peter whenever we planned to do something together. He's very creative, so he always had a good excuse, and he even believed the excuses himself. I finally said to him, "I won't agree to wait for you anymore. What you're saying to me by being late is that your time is more valuable than my time, which means you're more important than I am, and that is simply not true." He understood what I was saying and made an agreement not to be late anymore, or if he was, at least to call me and let me know—he has kept his agreement.

When we talked about his habit, he realized that he had grown up in a family that had very specific expectations for him, and these expectations did not align with his own dreams. He was forced, for a time, to put aside his talents and live his parents' ideas. He felt as though he had no control over anything in his life. Nothing was really his. So he found one thing he could have some control over, and that was time. Being late made him feel on an unconscious level that he had some power in his life. It was also a way of getting back at his parents. He unconsciously felt they had broken an agreement with him by refusing to see who he really was and insisting he become someone else. So he broke his agreements with them about time. When he recognized the origin of the habit, he realized that as an adult he could choose to express his power in other more conscious and more creative ways if he was willing to give up the need to control others through being late.

Find an area in your life where you feel a need to renegotiate an agreement, the same way my friend Peter did with time. See if you can find the origin of the agreement and how it may have served you in the past. Ask yourself what it is costing you in the present. Then ask yourself what you would gain and how your life would be different if you renegotiated the agreement.

CHAPTER TWELVE

Making Space

*A*N IMPORTANT PART of becoming a warrior is the ability to choose how we fill our lives. What will we allow in? What do we create space for? What do we shut out?

Perhaps the best illustration I can offer involves writing this book. When I first thought about writing it I felt very contracted. I wasn't sure I could come up with enough ideas to fill this many pages. But then I found a publisher who really wanted the book and they told me, "What you have to say is going to be important to a lot of people. You write it and we'll publish it." Soon after I was running with my dog, Shilo, trying to organize my thoughts and feeling totally inadequate to the job. I heard the voice inside me say, "You aren't going to write this book alone." I felt the space inside me shift and open up, and I knew the access to the ideas had just changed from limited to limitless. Now when I sit down to write, I thank the muses—indeed I am not alone: I get myself out of the way, the space opens, and the ideas flow in. I can't take all the credit for what happens then but I have agreed to take the responsibility.

In our workshops something similar occurs. We create the space for our students to experience themselves in a new way. Many of them have described this process as the creation of a space in themselves that feels completely empty, and at the same time feels very full. It is as if they have been empowered to make new choices about designing their lives all over again, this time according to what they want for themselves rather than what others want them to do or be. They take this feeling out into their lives as a touchstone, a new paradigm for their lives.

The weekend is a good model for illustrating what it's like to learn how to make space in order to create the quality of life we dream of having. During the process of the weekend, they are committed to finding their inner warrior. To do this they have to face their habitual selves, their fearful selves, all of the internal clamoring that keeps them from being in the silent space where they can hear the voice of the true Self. For many of our students, it is the hardest thing they have ever had to do. And when they break through all the old habits and clamorings, and experience the warrior space, they experience power and peace.

For perhaps the first time in their lives they experience themselves fully in the moment: present, alive, awake and aware, without the subliminal static that usually fills the space, and without the filters we usually drop between ourselves and reality. It takes a lot of courage to be who we really are, and see things the way they really are. But once you get a taste for what it's like to be awake, you'll literally fight not to go back to sleep.

We discover very quickly what it is that distracts us and lulls us into sleep. Clearly it's not the outside world that does it, at least it doesn't do it alone. The real culprit is the "monkey mind" which comes into play when we turn too much of our power over to our egos.

The monkey mind will do anything it can to keep you out of the present. It will keep you infinitely entertained and occupied, reviewing your past, rehearsing the future, whatever it takes to keep you out of This Moment Now, which is where your warrior lives. Because when your warrior shows up, your monkey mind shuts up.

Everything we've discussed so far in this book, from identifying where our energy is blocked, to keeping agreements, is focused now on this point. When your warrior is in its power, your monkey mind relinquishes control. It literally hands over the reins of control knowing it is in the presence of a superior power.

Many metaphysical systems teach that we have to destroy the ego to become enlightened. No wonder it puts up such a fuss! Would you go down without a fight? I have a slightly different way of looking at it, seeing the ego as an ally rather than an opponent to be destroyed. I believe we need our ego to negotiate our day-to-day reality. Someone has to balance the checkbook and get us to the hair dresser on time. But we can't depend only on our egos to tell us how to live our lives. The ego is motivated primarily by fear, and when left to its own devices will convince us that we can only be safe if we are in complete control of the world around us. The experience of love is foreign to it. This creates a very limited sense of reality because it leaves God and human intimacy out of the equation. When we only listen to the ego, we get the impression that there can't be a Higher Intelligence or Power greater than ourselves that we can trust. Give it too much space and the ego's monkey mind will clutter up our lives so that we forget why we are here. The ego knows that when we remember our life's purpose, and start listening to our Higher Self, we stop letting it (the ego) direct our lives. It's a little like a petty bureaucrat who runs amuck when he is given more power than he can handle, but because he likes having the power he doesn't want to give it up. We need to create the space for our egos to do just what they were intended to do, which is to *serve us* and *not run us*. This begins with identifying what the ego is good at and giving it responsibility for only what it can do well.

> The ego is meant to handle the details of our lives;
> To remind us of our anniversary, not pick our mates;
> To keep our appointment book up to date, not choose
>   our life's work;
> To balance the accounts, not try to tell us where our
>   supply comes from.

Above all, the ego's foundation is fear; working alone it can know nothing of love. And if you give it free rein it's monkey mind will clutter your life with all the products of fear, leaving no space for love and peace.

So where do we begin? How do we learn to recognize the difference between the voice of the ego and the voice of the Higher Self? We breathe ourselves into our bellies, we get quiet, and we allow our warrior to create the space for the voice of the Higher Self to come through. Sit quietly, relax your body, keep your back still, go into soft focus, keeping your awareness and your breath in your belly. If your attention wanders, slightly exaggerate your warrior breath and gently bring it back to your belly. At this point you can ask if you have a specific question of your Higher Self. Or you may choose to simply listen. Sometimes I hear a voice inside me, or sometimes I simply have a sense of a message being delivered, or of a new awareness.

When the voice of the ego is trying to talk to me, it feels like something from the outside trying to get in. When my Higher Self speaks to me, it's an experience of something from deep within coming out.

Intuition, those moments when we have a gut feeling, or have a dream that seems important, is a door to higher knowing. When we listen, really listen, we can hear the voice of our Higher Self.

For many people the voice of the ego has a jagged, frenetic feeling, often preoccupied with events not occurring in the present, while the voice of the Higher Self is one of a quiet excitement, focused in the here and now, peaceful and vibrant.

Always remember that the ego is the voice of the "old brain," sometimes referred to as the reptilian brain, which has limited focus and awareness. Reptile brain can't comprehend a Higher Self. The Higher Self, by contrast, can include the ego and its specialized responsibilities in its awareness, and is attuned to the bigger picture of our spiritual identity.

Remember that the ego will reach into its bag of tricks and create confusion, panic, and self-doubt in order to convince us that we must listen to it. If any of those are present, you know you are not in your belly.

We know that in the warrior's arsenal are the qualities of self-discipline, perseverance, and infinite patience. Once you've dedicated your path to the warrior rather than the ego, your warrior will just keep going after it until he gets the job done. And you feel the space in your heart start to open, you feel the space in your mind open, and you feel the space in your belly open, and you begin to feel your connection to All That Is. These are the moments of grace, when the space opens and God comes through, and we are given a taste of where our warrior's path is taking us.

What do we fill the space of our lives with? Do we use events, objects, people, or substances to enhance our connection with the present or distract ourselves from it? What voice do we hear from the television that's on eight hours a day? Does it support us to be awake or does it put us to sleep? Does it bring us into our reality, or does it take us away? Think about how much space in your life these hours represent, then ask if this is something you've openly chosen or simply allowed to happen.

Television and much of the print media encourage us to take the focus off ourselves and who we are. They encourage us to ignore the uncomfortable and dissonant conditions we have created in our lives, detach from our own reality and become voyeuristically absorbed in the lives of others.

Notice the key themes around which most television and film are built. The three V's: violence, victimization, and vengeance. This is all great entertainment for the ego, which is focused primarily on the drama of life as struggle and danger. At the other extreme there's the ego's avaricious nature and its fascination with and resentment of people who seem to have more than we have.

Instead of working for our own dreams we watch the dreams of others unfold. We unconsciously drift into the Celebrity syndrome, or the Jewish mother syndrome, or the stage parent, or the son who follows in his father's footsteps but never discovers his own path. A warrior knows that we are each an individual expression of the Divine. Warrior work is about finding our own path, developing our own gifts, and making our own unique contribution to our world.

*T*HIS IS YOUR LIFE: TAKE IT BACK

When you decide to take your life back, when you choose to have your power, there are three doors you will have to go through. They are the doors of anger, grief, and pain. If you say you don't have one of those, there is an additional door for you to look at. It's known as the door of denial. You'll have to go through that one first. We step through the door of denial by recognizing that there is a part of us that constantly struggles to prove that we know it all and are in complete control of our lives. Moving beyond this so that we can step through the door of denial requires two things: first, the recognition that denial is one of the favorite weapons of the ego, and second, a willingness to entertain the possibility that there might be another way to look at your life.

The three other doors will show up in different sequences, depending on your life experience.

The first door for me was anger, since I used it as a shield to keep myself safe. It kept me from feeling grief and pain, and it kept other people away. I also used my anger as a weapon to attack any and all perceived adversaries. If I felt threatened, I would lash out with my anger, and blast some-one back. Most people fear anger, it can be a form of violence, and they will back off if you direct it at them.

The next door for me was pain. Pain was what I was try-ing to protect with my anger. I opened it when I felt strong enough to experience it without blaming others and yet still holding them accountable. My pain door didn't open until I could allow myself to feel compassion for myself, rather than pity. When I had done enough work on my anger not to desire retribution or harm to others, only then could I let my pain come forward.

The final door for me was grief. When I was strong enough I went through that door. As I experienced my pain, I realized I had a choice about how to relate to it. I could act like a victim and brood over how hard my life had been, which would only attract more pain, or I could act like a war-rior and turn the adversity into an ally by finding the lessons to be learned from the painful experiences, and thereby assure myself that I wouldn't have to repeat them. Only then could I let myself feel my grief over the lost opportunities, the missed possibilities, the experiences of love and joy I'd been denied, and denied myself. I felt my grief until I could accept that what ultimately matters isn't the choices we've made in the past, but the opportunity we now have to use the space in our present lives.

The sequence is not the same for everyone. The final door is usually the most repressed, and the most difficult. Anger turns to rage, pain to suffering, grief to bereavement. Whatever we bury the deepest, and fear the most, is the hard-est to face.

With your warrior to support you, you'll go through a door when the space in your life is big enough to include that part of yourself, to own what's behind that door.

With courage, patience, and perseverance you'll know when you're ready to walk through each door. Then one day you will come to the final door, and step out into the vast landscape of your power.

Silence is one of the ways we can create space in our lives. Following an ancient practice, one of the great spiritual teachers, Babaji was silent for many years. Everything about his life was lean and spare. Nothing extra, no excesses, just this beautiful, bright being. One of the things he learned from the silence was to pare away the superfluous. His life was full of meaning, very immediate and very direct.

In everyday life few of us would be willing or able to take a vow of silence lasting many years, as Babaji did. However, we can still learn much about ourselves from silence by remaining silent for just one day. Communicate by writing what you want to say. It will make you have to look at what's coming out of your mouth. When it's over you'll be surprised at how much editing you'll want to do, cutting out everything but those words that convey your most essential truths and basic needs. And you will discover vast spaces opening up within you.

*T*HE WISDOM OF THE FAST

Fasting is another way to become acquainted with how we fill the space of our lives. I'm a pretty good cook, and I enjoy good food, but one of the times in my life that I felt the fullest was during a two-week fast.

Look at what goes in your mouth as well as what comes out. What do we fill our mouths and our bellies with? Do we create our meals consciously? Is food a way of sharing pleasure with others or do we stuff our faces as a way of filling the void in our lives? Notice when you use food as a drug, to numb your pain, anger, or grief. So much of the obesity in our world is an expression of denial, literally creating protective walls around our essential selves. Food is prasad, a gift from Grandmother Earth to her children, meant to delight and enliven us, not sedate and deaden us.

When you discover the space actually available to you, begin to examine how you are filling it. Make choices that will truly celebrate your life. Are you filling the space of your life with drugs, alcohol, loud music, sex (not lovemaking—which creates space—but hydraulics), or anything to clutter the senses or sensibilities so that there is no room for the message that waits to come through? Is there space to hear the voice that tells you where your fear lives, reminds you of where your work is? Is there space to hear the voice that says you are loved, the voice that says you are enough, the voice that says you have been given everything you need to do your work? If the space isn't there, make it. The warrior's path, everything we've explained in this book so far, provides you with all the tools you need for doing just that.

$\mathcal{S}$PACING OUT

As I write this, I'm sitting in a hotel room in Reno. We are here to teach a self-defense class for the medical students at the University of Nevada. Fourteen floors below me is a casino. The entire psychic space in the casino is comprised of noise and neon. There is nothing in that room that even approximates a sound, shape, or color that exists in nature. Everyone there looks like a zombie, enclosed in a psychic sack that cuts them off from everyone else.

My own psyche rebels, telling me to get out of this place. I feel bombarded. My nervous system feels hammered and my second chakra has been on red alert ever since we got here. It's exhausting.

This environment is an exaggeration of what we do as a culture, which is to fill the space with so much stimulation that we finally space out and don't feel anything.

I recently had an incident occur that served as a teaching for me, motivating me to look at a part of my life I had been neglecting and had been refusing to make space for. I woke up in the middle of the night with my left eye hurting badly. I wear extended wear contact lenses for convenience. But with an infection in my eye, I was unable to wear them for three days. I'm very nearsighted and without my lenses I am nearly helpless. I had to sit with that helplessness for three days and in that time I realized that the part of myself that was constantly guarding the gates was terrified because I couldn't see. What if the Mongolian hordes showed up before I could put my lenses back on? Who, if not me, would hold them back? From deep in my solar plexus, all the old terror that I had experienced as a child began to emerge. I realized I had never given this terror any space. It had been particularly important in my early life to deny this terror, otherwise it would have taken us down. That inner child was doing what she had to do to get my attention. She knew my life was big enough and safe enough now to make room for her, to sit with her fear until she felt safe. I realized that I had abandoned her so that I could become the grown-up to guard the gates. There hadn't been anyone else to do that in my childhood. But the gates had now swung open, and the Mongolian hordes were pitching their yurts, feeding their horses, and singing around their open fires.

And the voice inside me said, "I AM eternally vigilant for you."

And I knew that my inner child is safe, and I am free of the exhausting job of always being vigilant.

So what parts of yourself have you abandoned? Your grief, your anger, your pain, your ability to play, to dance, to make a mistake, to laugh? Is there enough space in your life now to include what you have cast out? Give yourself space to let it in now.

One of the ways we can make the space is to let ourselves care more. It's a risky path and not without pitfalls and pratfalls. But as we open ourselves up to care for others, we open up to caring for ourselves.

- *Visit a nursing home.* Sit with the grandparents no one wants anymore.
- *Visit an animal shelter.* Spend some time with the animals that have been thrown away. Take one home.

- *Visit a prison.* Spend time with the part of ourselves we are punishing.
- *Volunteer some time at an AIDS hospice.* Spend some time with the part of ourselves we are banishing.
- *Spend some time on the street talking to homeless people.*

These are our castoffs, our refuse. In a very real way they are the abandoned parts of ourselves. We have cast them out, cut them off, banished them, punished them; these are the parts of ourselves that we fear. These are our shadows.

If we cannot make the space for them in our lives, they operate outside the realm of our control, and show up when and where we least expect them. They stalk us. When we stop acknowledging them, when we disown them and cast them out of our lives, they become dangerous. They start taking up more space in our lives. They lead us into the darkness, often against our will, and in ways we don't even recognize:

> We get mugged.
> We get old.
> We get bitten.
> We get fired.
> We step in a pile of shit.
> We get AIDS.
> We end up pushing a shopping cart.

When we can acknowledge our shadow aspects, through caring for those in our society who carry them, we almost magically free ourselves of their influence. Our shadow aspects dissolve and in the space we've created we discover our warrior.

Sometimes the spaces we create are very mundane and practical. What do you have that you no longer need, but which someone else can use? Start with your closet or your garage. Watch what comes in when you give away what you no longer want or need, thus making a new space in your life. A friend of mine told me how she recently emptied out a thirty-year-old accumulation of "stuff" in her garage, donating it to the various service organizations who could benefit from it. She converted her garage to a studio where she is now painting. For years, she had been putting off her artwork because she didn't have the "space" for it. It took her awhile to set up her studio, even after she had cleared out the garage because she didn't want to have to admit to herself that all those years she'd had everything she needed. Today, she is painting, having made the space to pursue a gift she'd neglected far too long.

Make space for animals and flowers and creativity in your life. Insist on beauty and laughter. Simplify and surround yourself with treasures. You'll soon discover that elegance is another word for simplicity.

How do you fill your time? Time is the measurement of movement, and self-expression. The most effective movement is elegant. In an effective self-defense system, initial movement is,

- Striking surface directly to target area, no telegraphing (hesitating, posturing, bluffing, no fooling)
- Using the least amount of effort (no flailing, struggling, no force against force), fully committed (no quitting)
- Doing only what it takes to get the job done (no equivocating)
- Following the flow of energy to the target area (no resisting)

What don't you have enough of? What will you have
     to empty out so that it can come in?
In order to make the space for money to come in, we
     have to empty out fear of lack.
To make the space for love to come in, we have to
     empty out selfishness, and self-hatred.
To make the space for our life's work to come in, we
     have to empty out self-doubt.

To make the space for joy to come in, we have to
empty out self-pity.
To make the space for our power to come in, we
have to empty out our fear.

The warrior creates a safe space for us to encounter our
fear, gives us the courage to face it, the strength to overcome
it, and the wisdom to choose how else we want to fill the
space.

As you pursue this process, remember the three doors for
accomplishing this:

1. *The Door of Anger*—acknowledging the anger we are
   feeling because of something we presently believe
   has limited our lives.
2. *The Door of Pain*—acknowledging the pain we are
   feeling as a wound we experienced in our past.
3. *The Door of Grief*—acknowledging the grief we feel
   as a result of lost opportunities, or joy we were
   denied as children, or the grief that we have denied
   ourselves as a result of the belief systems we created
   to protect ourselves from feeling our anger or our
   pain.

And of course, let's not forget the Door of Denial. (What
denial?) Unless we open our eyes to that one, we'll never get
close enough to open the other three.

Making space in our lives to do the things we truly want
to do, things that satisfy us at a deep spiritual level, rather
than just at the ego level, is the very essence of freedom. It is
the ability to know what gives our lives meaning and purpose
and then creating the room and the energy to make it happen.

CHAPTER THIRTEEN

Getting What We Want

*T*HINGS ARE THE WAY they are because we want them that way." Most of us struggle with this idea. But it is an essential concept for the warrior to master and if we are truly going to come into our own power, we need to look at this idea closely. Desire has the power to create. This observation comes under the heading of Universal law number two, Take Responsibility.

Consciousness creates, that is an ineffable truth. As warriors we are bringing the level of our lives up to conscious choice: first by taking responsibility for our presently unconscious choices and then by paying more attention to how and why we are making those choices.

We can better understand our choices by paying attention to our thoughts. To do this, notice your daydreams and fantasies; pay attention to the subliminal messages running through your head, the nagging voice in the back of your mind or the gentle pull you might feel toward another person or situation, or the anxiety you feel in situations that seem benign enough on the surface. Listen to the voices whispering just at the periphery of your consciousness. This takes some

effort on our part, of course. Most of us don't hear these subliminal messages at all, having been conditioned to discount
them as *only in your mind.* The warrior quickly learns that
these kinds of messages can make a huge difference in our
lives, sometimes even making the difference between life and
death. Sometimes these messages come in the form of a "gut"
feeling, sometimes they are entire scenarios with characters
and events, as dramatic as a movie or novel.

My daydreams and fantasies often involve someone who
looks suspiciously like Sheena, Queen of the Jungle, rescuing
some helpless critter or hapless human from their evil tor-
mentors. She bravely faces insurmountable odds, using her
wits and her extraordinary martial arts skills to defeat the vil-
lains, and kick their butts. And then I wonder why I create
occasional conflict in my life!

Truly this fantasy mirrors my early life experience and
tends to keep me focused on situations that in some way echo
those same old themes. With this focus I am likely to notice
and respond to helpless beings in distress. My fantasies are
like magnets, drawing these situations in. And unless I take
responsibility for this process, I may see only these same
themes in life, projected from my inner world to the outer
world. I may even create these themes in actual situations
that would seem to justify my feelings and actions.

It's like visiting a mental video game arcade. It may be
infinitely fascinating and mesmerizing, but it also may keep
me out of the place that is grounded in present reality. The
more energy we invest in a thought, the more likely it is to
manifest, which is the way visualizations work. Or the more a
thought is repeated, the more likely it is to be manifest in the
outer world, which is the way a mantra works. One of the
things warrior work is about is staying in the present, that is,
staying in our bellies, and learning to focus our thoughts so
that we create consciously. That way we don't have to run
around cleaning up the fallout from our unconscious mani-
festations. For example, if you spend thirty minutes a day in
meditation, repeating, "I have abundance and prosperity!"
and the other twenty-three-and-a-half hours being bombarded

by the unconscious messages that say, "I'll never have enough money. How am I going to pay my bills? I don't deserve to have wealth. I hope that check doesn't bounce. I can't afford it," what do you think will show up in your life?

I believe things are accelerating in our world and wanting for ourselves alone, with no regard for how it may impact others has become a luxury we can no longer afford. We need to pay much more attention to the inner worlds we create, and choose between letting them shape our life experience or learning about the Universal principles that affect all our lives. We have to ask:

- Does it serve me?
- Does it serve others?
- Does it serve Grandmother Earth?

If you miss on any of the three you may be able to get what you want, but you may find in the long run that it isn't worth the price you have to pay. We may want to have a wonderful home, but if we cut down all the giant redwoods to do that we'll decimate our forests with all the attendant problems that go with deforestation.

We are being forced to look at the bigger picture, the ripple effect of our actions, thoughts, and desires. We can't make a step of progress in our own lives without taking everyone else with us. We don't make a retrograde step without dragging everyone else back. What the warrior knows is that we are all part of the same Self. The spiritual principles that teach us to see the whole in an unselfish way are ultimately self-empowering in ways that seem unimaginable to the mind ruled only by the ego. The moments of epiphany in my life when I experienced my connection to all things and knew myself to be part of a greater whole, allowed me to step out of the box my ego had created and shifted my perspective so that to act without regard for others no longer made any sense to me. One of the messages the warrior has to deliver is to honor our connection to All That Is by acting unselfishly, and responsibly, even when it is a hard choice to do so.

We have been living on borrowed resources, because we have put our faith in fear and limitation, which are the central values we see when we look only through the eyes of the ego. The bill has come due, and either we are going to pay it or our kids are. Just contemplating the national debt is enough to make you want to put your head in the sand (which is how we created the debt in the first place). When the warrior in us gets driven underground, what takes over is the belief that we have to grab whatever we can because there isn't enough in the present to go around. So we have to borrow from the future. Since the unconscious knows there is only the present, the message is that this is a limited, stingy, finite Universe, and we'll never have what we want unless we steal it from someplace else. Driven by fear that we won't have what we need, or want, we ransom the future, stealing from generations not yet born.

The warrior knows, however, God is not stingy.

You've probably noticed that as you have become more conscious, more aware, the consequences of your thoughts and actions manifest more quickly. I believe this is happening globally. Things are accelerating on both an individual and collective basis. The level of the game is up, we're playing for very big stakes. The Universe is not cutting us much slack.

I believe that one of the purposes of living in an apparent cause and effect physical universe is to teach us how we create our reality with thought and action over time. Like playing with clay. Ultimately we discover that when we are fully awake and aware there is no lapse between the first desire that gives rise to thought, and manifestation. Like playing with light.

Just as the weakness and vulnerability of the ego comes out of fear and a belief of lack or limitation, so the strength of the warrior comes from an understanding of the bounty of God's gifts to us all. We are learning that while the ego seeks gratification in material objects, the warrior looks beyond the material to seek spiritual fulfillment. A warrior knows that what God desires for us is much greater than anything the ego can ever imagine.

For the warrior there are two parts to making choices. First, we must ask, "What do we want to have?" And, second, "What do we want to change?" Let's explore these.

What Do You Want?

I recommend that you take a piece of paper and do the following exercise. Write down a description of everything you want, leaving room to briefly answer the following questions:

- How does it serve me?
- How does it serve others?
- How does it serve Grandmother Earth?

If what you want doesn't serve all three, ask yourself what it will take to bring it into alignment. Of course, if it doesn't align, you can choose to have it anyway by mashing it into shape. I spent a lot of my life subscribing to the school of If-All-Else-Fails-Use-Force. However, the results from such a strategy for life are short term, and exhausting. We invariably end up putting out huge amounts of energy to get things that don't satisfy us in the long run and sometimes turn out to be downright disastrous. The warrior thinks long term, and in the process of doing so realizes his or her power in ways that the ego-driven soldier mentality never can.

The warrior knows that alignment is effortless, that it provides energy and a sense of fulfillment that can be achieved in no other way.

To our list of wants we might add an additional question: Can I want this for everyone? "Well of course not! I wouldn't give a Ferrari to a three-year-old!" you might reply. To phrase this question in a slightly different way, try taking the object, or concept, of your desire to its spiritual equivalent. For example, what does the Ferrari represent? Perhaps freedom or mobility. Similarly, maybe that new house represents a sense of inner peace, home, or family. New clothes might be seen as expressing beauty. An object is often a symbol of a

larger idea. As warriors we explore what that symbol represents in the bigger picture. For instance, money by itself can't
make you happy; but what money represents, such as freedom and choice, or the ability to pursue an activity that you
feel is meaningful, does have the possibility of making you
happy.

Can you want that for everyone? If the answer is yes,
then you should have it.

*W*HAT DO YOU WANT TO CHANGE?

In the same way that you made a list of your wants, make a
list of the things you would like to change. Here's a simple
exercise. Choose an area in your life that you would like to
change. Keep it simple, but pick something that is important
to you, such as:

- I'd like to have a more loving relationship.
- I'd like to have more money.
- I'd like my career to be something I love.

Now, state what you have to gain by changing. For example, "If I had more money I'd be able to travel, which has
always been one of my dreams." With that done, write down
what you have to lose, or give up, if this should happen. For
example, "I'm afraid I'd have to take on more responsibility
and stress if I earned more money." What holds the existing
system in place will usually show up on the "What-I-have-to-
lose" list. These are the payoffs, what you get by keeping the
habit in place.

For example, if you got into a better relationship, where
you experienced more love and reciprocity, maybe you would
have to give up your victim role, from which you've always
gotten a lot of sympathy from your friends.

To give up not having enough money, you'd have freedom
and ease in your life. But maybe you would have to relinquish
the belief in the nobility of poverty and struggle. To give up

not having work you love, you'd get joy and creativity. But maybe you'll have to give up blaming others for keeping you from your dreams.

Remember, the system got set in place because at some point it served you or protected you. By asking what you'd give up you get to decide if it has outgrown its usefulness.

Maybe you aren't ready to be independent. You discover you still need to be taken care of. Maybe you still need to experience crisis to feel alive. Maybe you aren't yet clear about your dreams.

In order for me to give up my investment in struggle, I had to give up my beliefs that nothing was freely given, that I had to fight for whatever I got. I had to give up the notion that there was some value in proving my martyrdom. What I eventually got when I did let go of these illusions was a brand new sense of peace, ease, self-acceptance, not feeling separate, the knowledge that I was a warrior.

To recognize our choices—what we have to give up if we want to change—puts us in a place of power. Without blame or putting ourselves down, we can fully *own* what we are doing and decide whether or not that behavior or belief system still serves us.

Christ was a great warrior. He fearlessly fought for his beliefs, and stood in his truth even when he had to stand alone.

Christ's first and last teachings, or miracles, had to do with creating what we want. The first was the wedding feast, where Mary, the voice of the Feminine, said to him, "They're running out of wine. Why don't you turn a couple of barrels of this water into a nice Cabernet." He answered, " No, I'm not ready." She said, "Trust yourself, don't even think about it. You are ready." He said, "Listen, I'm really not ready." She said, "Stop kvetching, get out of your head and just do it." And He did. And everyone continued to have a good time.

His last demonstration of supply was the loaves and fishes. From apparent lack he created plenty because he knew he was always connected to Source. He had no bank account, no credit cards, nothing stashed away for a rainy day, because he knew that in every present moment his every need was met. There is no need to hoard anything if you know you have everything.

When He said, "And greater works shall you do," who do you think He was talking about? If the voice in your head is saying, "He can't mean me," ask yourself. Whose voice is that?

> If not you, who?
> If not now, when?

The principle is simple, we are never separate from Source. How do we know this? Because we are alive.

Demonstrating supply has been one of my toughest lessons because, more than anything, it is a lesson in trust. It is having to rely on something other than myself, bigger than myself, to take care of me. Knowing my story I'm sure you can see how I developed this habit, that it is something I learned, not a truth about the way the universe really is. That which created me sustains me, if I let it, and even if I don't.

Getting what we want is about surrender, about turning it over. It is about giving up control. It is about understanding that you have to give it up before you can get it. As one of my teachers once told me, "The job of the Divine Mother is already taken in this Universe. Besides, there is a waiting list for that position and there are a whole lot of people ahead of you."

My warrior had to overcome the belief that there are forces in the universe that are bigger than me that meant me harm. And my warrior had to accept in faith that there are forces in the universe bigger than me that mean me well.

When we are totally immersed in the belief systems of the physical world, cause and effect appear to rule our lives. For example, it becomes very easy to say, and be completely convinced, that we can't have a nice home because we can't afford one. But as we shift out of limited, cause-effect thinking, the warrior begins to recognize a higher truth. The warrior moves toward the realization that our minds are God's

Mind. That means we can have anything that the Mind of God includes.

We can have whatever we want as long as we want nothing more than we want union with God. Seek first the Kingdom, and everything else will be added. At this level, we perhaps begin to understand our desire as prayer.

*T*RY THIS

Sit quietly for one minute. Write down, without editing, changing, or judging your stream of consciousness. Write down everything that comes into your mind. When you are done, read it and see what you are saying to yourself. Do these thoughts support what you think your goals are, or do they get in the way?

The purpose of individual will, one of your warrior qualities, is to discipline the conscious mind, to use your boundary-setting skills to gently correct a thought or belief that no longer serves you. To help you Pay Attention, without judgment or condemnation, to what you are saying to yourself, what you are asking for. To notice your thoughts before they manifest themselves.

I spent years feeling overworked because not only did I set up and teach the workshops, I also handled all the other related aspects of the business, many of which I am not very good at. I kvetched, but I couldn't seem to create for myself someone who would help me with the parts of the business I thought I was ready to turn over. I started to pay attention to what the fearful voice of my ego was continually whispering just at the periphery of my consciousness. Now, the ego's reasons were convincing, "How can I afford it?" "No one else understands this business better than I do." I realized that in order to get the help I needed, I would have to give up control of an idea that I had birthed, nurtured, and spent a lifetime creating. I had to remind myself that the idea for the workshops may have come through me, but it didn't come from me. Allowing myself to be taken care of in this instance also meant letting a work that impacted a lot of other people, be taken care of as well. Soon after this realization one of our graduates, Mari, called us and asked to meet with us. During the meeting Mari told us that the workshop had changed her life, she was leaving a successful career in the legal field, and she wanted to work for us. She said she knew we couldn't afford her full time, and she was willing to start wherever we were comfortable. She said she knew we needed her and this work was her right work. She began by handling the business details better than I ever did, and by assisting in the workshops. She has since earned her black belt, taken over a lot of the teaching in the workshops, and teaches our five hour workshop on her own. She has found her place in the work, her talent continues to unfold, and the support she gives me is immeasurable. In order for me to get what I wanted I had to give up Doing-It-All-Myself, I had to give up control. What I got when I was able to do this was time, freedom, increased business, support, and I got to extend our *family*.

CHAPTER FOURTEEN

Respect

*T*HE LESSON OF RESPECT is a critical teaching in the education of a warrior. Without respect learning can't take place. Without respect the center won't hold. Without respect we can't establish a productive and creative relationship to Source, ourselves, each other, or our world.

In the martial arts, respect has a special meaning. It is holding the teacher in high esteem, recognizing that he or she has dedicated usually many years, sometimes a lifetime to his or her work. We must choose our teachers wisely, committing ourselves for a period of time to their teachings. It is because we respect who they are and what they know that we can trust them to communicate their knowledge to us, and quite literally, to be responsible for our safety.

In warrior work we begin with respect for Source. We honor our Origin and Universal Law, knowing that by doing so we can come into alignment and live our lives with greater ease and harmony. When we don't respect this law we invite chaos; our lives are difficult and often painful, serving as a reminder to seek realignment. For example, by honoring the Law of Love, our lives become increasingly expansive; by

disrespecting this law, our lives become small and contracted. The Law of Love is built on the principle that the
others' welfare is important to us and we take great pleasure
from having them in our life. By respecting the Law of Take
Responsibility, our lives become our own creation; by disrespecting it we give our power away, becoming victims of cir-
cumstance. By respecting the Law of Pay Attention, we stay
in the present, awake and aware; by disrespecting it, we are
constantly scrambling to keep up with reality, or getting
blindsided by it.

In respecting ourselves, we care for our bodies, honoring
them as a gift from the Divine Mother. We treat them as pre-
cious since they are only on loan. We are conscious about
what we eat; we find some sort of exercise or art form that
keeps us feeling like a finely tuned instrument, so that we
may experience joy with inhabiting the physical self. We
learn to defend ourselves, so that we are physically safe. We
honor our sexuality, knowing that there is a lot more to sex
than nerve endings. Sex is one of the ways we can truly connect with each other, and through each other, with God. It is a
taste of bliss.

In respecting each other, as we do when we respect Universal Law, we are willing to see each other clearly, without
judgment. We honor each other's beliefs, learn each other's
history, and respect each other's boundaries. Respect creates
the matrix for a healthy family dynamic by honoring the
autonomy of each individual and acting with the awareness
of how our actions will affect the other members of our family. Respect allows individuals to come together and function
as a group. The prime directive for respect is *with harm to
none*. We respect our grandparents as keepers of wisdom and
experience; we respect our children as keepers of trust and
innocence; we respect our mates as mirrors, for our own
growth and wisdom. Lack of respect is, I believe, where it has
broken down for us as a society. When we are respectful, it is
impossible to put our needs or desires ahead of anyone else's.
Indeed, working for the common good becomes reflexive and
natural.

In our workshops, which serve as a model for community for the participants, respect is essential to maintain safety, and to create a context for learning to take place. One form of respect expressed in the workshop is discipline. By creating boundaries, rules and laws, we establish a safe place for the physical work that is potentially dangerous. It requires everyone's agreement. Respect is never blind obedience; that would be tyranny. When that agreement is broken the possibility for injury exists.

Students respect their teachers. They honor the time and effort their instructors put into mastering the system they now teach. Teachers respect their students. They honor the openness and willingness and trust students bring to the work so that they can receive the teaching. Instructors also respect the fact that our students are our teachers and that together we comprise the never-ending chain of learning.

For a warrior, respect begins with our relationship to Grandmother Earth. The reason our respect begins here has to do with the fact that without the support of the earth we can't survive. Just as the health of an infant is dependent on the health of the mother, so our well-being is dependent on the health of Grandmother Earth. Without this basic understanding the warrior's training is incomplete. This knowledge begins with our respect for the five kingdoms on Grandmother Earth:

1. *The Mineral Kingdom, the bones of Grandmother Earth.*
   Rumor has it that there has been underwater nuclear testing in the Baltic sea which has torn a hole in the earth's core. This has been done ostensibly by the Russians, but it could just as easily have been us. This is clearly a display of tremendous disrespect for our planet, and all the inhabitants who will most certainly be impacted by this action. At the opposite extreme, those who resist strip-mining for various minerals are expressing a respect for this part of Grandmother Earth. We can see from these examples

that respect is not only an expression of courtesy, but when carried out into the big picture it can spell our survival. This goes back to one of the earlier principles we discussed, a warrior knows that all actions have consequences and that there are no isolated acts.

2. *The Plant Kingdom, the lungs of Grandmother Earth.*
As I write this, one of the last stands of ancient redwood trees is being slaughtered to make patio furniture. Those trees don't belong to the lumber company; they belong to Grandmother Earth and we were to hold them in trust for our children, and our children's children to enjoy. A thousand years gone in a matter of minutes to be sliced up for decking. Those who protest such abuse of our forests, and who are contributing both their resources and their labor to plant new trees, not only recognize our interdependence but also demonstrate their respect through their actions.

3. *The Kingdom of the Oceans and the Waters, the blood of Grandmother Earth.*
In virtually every city across the nation, our water has become polluted with chemicals and organic material, to say nothing of the chemicals that get dumped in the water to make it "safe." There aren't many places we can safely swim anymore, we certainly can't safely drink water. We're using our waters as a toilet and forcing its inhabitants to live in it. This could never have come about had there been respect for the gift of water and our dependence on it.

4. *The Animal Kingdom, the heart of Grandmother Earth.*
We have chased the wild animals out of their homes, left no safe place for them to run or fly. Millions of

species are dying, and we are breaking Grandmother's heart. And we wonder why she is taking
matters into her own hands. To show respect would
be to stop and consider—with deep love—the welfare
of all the animals affected anytime we press into
their habitat to build a highway, expand a city, clear
land for any purpose, or set up new airline routes
which could affect wildlife.

5. *The Human Kingdom.*
   Guess which kingdom could disappear from the face
   of the planet without disturbing the balance among
   the other kingdoms? There's only one Kingdom out
   of the five. It is ironical that our self-respect is a key
   to the respect of the other four. Were we to fully
   respect ourselves we could not abuse or ignore the
   destruction of the others. We would be unable to see
   them as something less than ourselves, which is how
   the fearful ego objectifies, and, thereby, justifies the
   abuse. We would remember that we are all part of
   the same Self, incapable of not feeling each other's
   pain or joy, on some level.

We were entrusted with this beautiful planet. And we are
supposed to participate in its evolution, not chop it up and
sell the pieces. Did we really think we could get away with it?

A warrior knows that without respect there can be no
learning, and without learning, the process of entropy and
disintegration begins, not only on an individual level but on a
collective, global level as well.

The apocalypse has already begun. Look around. Read the
paper. Watch the news. The prophesies are coming true. It's
not too late to turn it around, unless we continue to ignore the
signs. We are like lemmings headed for the cliff in a huge, collective march of denial, afraid to look at what we've done or
where we're going. A warrior knows confrontation conquers
fear and so a warrior cuts a path through all illusions of denial.

The consequences of our present actions will reach far into the future, either making life worse, or making it better for those who follow us.

As we develop respect for all life, including our own, we can take back our world. We can take it back from big business and big government, who are like Nero playing while Rome burns. By turning our power over to these institutions we have abdicated responsibility. We can't afford to do that anymore, it's not worth the price we are paying. It's costing us our self-respect. It's costing us our lives. It's costing us our world. Without this total expression of respect—in our relationship with each other, Grandmother Earth, and ultimately ourselves—we are victims, not warriors.

Warriors walk the world with respect, taking only what they can use, using only what they can replace. For those who have gone before them, warriors have gratitude. For those who travel with them, warriors have respect. For those who come after them, warriors leave this planet a better place. Warriors work to replenish and not to diminish.

We have attempted to tame everything, sanitize everything. That's an expression of *control over* others, an expression of fear and lost respect. We've forgotten how to get down and roll in the dirt, get up, shake ourselves off and howl, respecting and celebrating all of life, not just the parts we can dominate.

Respect is honoring each part of creation for exactly who or what it is. Including ourselves. It seems that having lost respect we believe we must impose our will on everything around us. If something doesn't fit our pictures, or gets in the way of our idea of civilization:

> We shoot it,
> Pave it over,
> Cut it down,
> Stuff it into panty hose,
> Stuff it into a suit,
> Put it in a ghetto,
> Move it to a reservation,

> Cage it in a zoo,
> Pretend it isn't there.

Respect is understanding that the Universe is a big enough place to include all of its ideas. A warrior understands that it is the quality of respect that brings harmony, and that it is the job of the warrior to keep harmony.

A good measure for respect is knowing that we don't have the right to do anything, or take anything, at the expense of anyone or anything else.

I've never been much of a camper. As much as I love being outdoors, I also like to be able to come inside when it gets too hot or too cold, or escape the mosquitoes when they come out. One of the best teachings for me in how disconnected from nature I had become was several years ago at a warrior retreat held in high desert, in mid-August. I was there to teach women's self-defense. I arrived the evening before the retreat was to begin. I set up my tent, put carpets on the floor, made my bed with matching comforter and pillows on one side of the tent, a coordinated bed for my Doberman on the other side, set up my bookshelf by subject and author, hung my lanterns, folded my clothes neatly in a dresser made from boxes, covered the boxes with a tapestry, and organized my kitchen with ice chest, pantry, propane stove, utensils, including a garlic press. I tucked us in for the night, covered my dog (she hated to be too cold, or hot) and climbed under my blankets that matched the rug and tapestry. I woke up thinking, "This isn't too bad, I won't miss too many of my creature comforts," climbed out of my tent to take a shower (armed with my hair dryer), and was greeted with howls of laughter.

The trade-off for no blow-drying was the wonderful companionship of living in close community, sharing meals (the garlic press came in very handy), sharing time, singing, laughing, drumming, getting grubby. (Thank God there was running water and two showers for forty women—but since I was the instructor, I gave myself a head start for the shower when I dismissed my class. I never said I was completely reformed.) During the day I watched the hawks soar. At night I stared at stars that seemed close enough to touch. Not a bad deal.

The experience taught me that I had gotten out of alignment, that I had tried to make the world fit my pictures instead of finding how I fit in the world. It was a lesson in respect.

From *The I Ching,* Hexagram 25, Innocence:

> When movement follows the law of heaven, man
> is innocent and without guile. His mind is natural
> and true, unshadowed by reflection or ulterior
> design. Nature that is not directed by spirit is not
> true, but degenerate nature. Man has received from
> heaven a nature innately good to guide him in all his
> movements. By devotion to this divine spirit within
> himself, he attains an unsullied innocence that leads
> him to do right with instinctive sureness and with-
> out any ulterior thought of reward and personal
> advantage.*

A good place to begin practicing respect is with our loved ones, looking at them in a new way, cherishing their lives, respecting their needs, even respecting what we consider their annoying habits or behaviors. Learning respect can begin with the people we work with, really noticing the contributions they make with their efforts, and the places where your efforts combine. It can begin with the way we treat other drivers in traffic, giving them space rather than competing for every break in traffic. We can pay attention to what we waste preparing meals for ourselves or our families, looking for ways to minimize the trash we dump out onto Grandmother

---

* *The I Ching: The Book Of Changes.* The Richard Wilhelm Translation. Bollingen Series, Princeton University Press. Richard Wilhelm, I Ching: The Book of Changes, trans. (Princeton: Princeton University Press; Bolligen Series XIX, 1960)

Earth. If we all had to be responsible for our own garbage for just one month, it would be a crash course in respect. We can begin by paying attention to resources we use that we fail to replace. As we increase our respect in these ways, interesting things begin to happen; we feel a growing sense of inner strength and begin to honor the power each of us has to change the world. We see that it is not only possible, but we are actually contributing to the creation of a world of warriors rather than a world of soldiers and victims. Every gesture of respect takes us closer to that goal, whether our efforts are realized immediately or not.

CHAPTER FIFTEEN

Letting It In

*A*N IMPORTANT ASPECT of becoming a warrior is the ability to *let it in.* We live in an abundant and loving Universe. We have been given everything we need to be happy and fulfilled. We can have anything we want. Then why don't we have it? What stands in the way of having what we want? The short answer is, "our tyrants."

It is both ironic and somehow very prophetic that as I sit here there are many extraordinary gifts that I find I must make a deliberate effort to take in. Writing them down as part of this chapter certainly serves to remind me of the importance of this warrior skill.

The laptop computer I wrote this book on was lent to me by my friend Jane. I had never used a computer and was writing the book by hand, which Jane pointed out to me, would take me to the next millennium, well past my deadline! Jane's generosity made my life a whole lot easier.

In the midst of the rush to meet my publisher's deadline, I forget to let in what is made available to me every day on this planet.

I'm sitting in my home in Marin County, in a wonderful house perched up in the hills like an eagle's nest. This house came to us as a gift from the Universe four years ago. Our friend, Leslie Duncan, who is a real estate broker, found it for us. It is twice as much house as the one we had been in, and we were able to buy it without increasing our mortgage payments. With the profit from this house, I was able to buy a home in Carmel Valley that is a dream come true for me.

I must admit there have been times in my past when my ego argued that opportunities like this only happened to others. But it isn't true. The only thing standing between me and these opportunities was me and my ability to let them in.

Hal Bennett and Susan Sparrow agreed to publish this book through their company, Tenacity Press. Who said you couldn't mix business and pleasure?

A year ago it wouldn't have seemed possible, but today I am sitting here writing this book. Once again I'm struck with the realization that we are always surrounded by everything we need to fulfill our dreams, if only we can learn to let it in.

In February of this year, I was awarded my 6th degree black belt. My sensi, Doug, continues to amaze me with his psychic tracking devices, and his confidence in me. Although I've worked hard for this, none of it would have been possible without the ability to take it in, to receive the gifts of the many teachers I've found, or who have found me through the years.

When Robert Humphrey passed away, the level of loss was so unacceptable, Patrick and I knew we had to find a way to keep our connection with him. We could not conceive of making the rest of the journey without him, so we had to find a new way to take it with him, a way not defined by our senses or confined in time and space. This meant walking our talk in a whole new way. This meant letting it in, in a whole new way. This was a whole new episode of Father Knows Best, of not my will but Thy Will. We learned that whatever you don't put on the altar gets taken, and whatever you put on the altar gets returned tenfold. Through this experience we were lifted to the next level of our unfoldment and our work, and Robert was the bridge from here to there. We knew the bridge was trust. We realized that it is not God's job to make sense to our human senses; it's God's job, like a Zen Master, to blow our minds right out of sensory illusion. Robert is an excellent koan. We were reminded of the story told by Swami Muktananda when he was on his death bed. His students surrounded him and cried, "Babaji! Babaji! please don't leave us!" He looked at them and said, "Leave you, where would I go?"

And we have let Christopher and Joel into our experience.

So what does the warrior have to do with all this?

Before I could let any of these gifts in, I had to face the inner tyrant who says, "You don't deserve this." I also had to face the tyrant who whispers, "This is too easy, something's wrong here." I had to face the tyrant who says, "You can't afford it," or "You don't have enough time." And face the tyrant who holds the other shoe, while I wait for the shoe to drop.

Because of the way I grew up, I developed the habit of never asking for help. My credo was to do it all myself, to refuse help even when others offered it. Every time I violated this internal agenda, disaster struck. More often than not, it wasn't just a shoe that dropped, the hammer dropped.

In this section I keep thinking about that old spiritual teaching about the man in the flood. You know, the flood waters are rising all around him and the man prays, "God, I have been your loyal servant all these years. Please save me from the flood." God answers, "Don't worry, I won't let you down." Nevertheless, the waters continue to rise. Finally, the man is on the roof of his house with water up to the eaves. A man comes along on a raft. "Come down from the roof and I'll take you to safety," he says. "No," the man on the roof says, "I'll trust God." A little while later a rescue boat arrives but again the man on the roof says, "No. I am a religious man. I will trust in God." A third rescuer comes along, this time in a helicopter. By now most of the roof is underwater and the house has left its foundation. But the man says, "No. I will trust in God." Moments later the house collapses from the force of the flood. The man drowns and goes off to Heaven.

He meets God and says, "God, I trusted you! You said you'd save me, what's the deal here?" God replies, "Look, first I sent you a man on a raft, then a rescue boat, and finally a helicopter!" The lesson of, course, is that it's all a gift from God. We need to recognize this to take it in. This man's tyrant came in the form of his limiting the form the gift would take.

When we believe in tyrants they appear in many different forms, always threatening to take away the gifts the Universe offers. I can say this with some authority since my warrior has had to learn many lessons to become adept at handling the tyrants I create. Let me offer you just a sampling.

I went to pick up the computer from Jane, and when I got in the car to leave, the battery had gone dead. My tyrants were saying, "Watch out! There's always a price to pay." I had stopped to have the car washed on the way. After all, I didn't want to bring her computer home in a car that was hip deep in dog hair. And the car wash guys left the lights on. (See, I told you it wasn't my fault.) However the tyrant's timing was slightly off; I already had the computer. Jane and I had to ask a man to help us start the car. So much for feminism.

Similarly, when we were in the process of buying our present house, the house we were selling fell out of escrow, leaving a pile of reports that identified a drainage problem that as it turned out didn't really exist. So Bob dug an unnecessary drainage ditch. Then, the seller couldn't find the deed for the new house on the day escrow was to close. They told us we couldn't move in until it was found, but we were already mostly out of the old house, and had to move in. My warrior guided me past that tyrant too. We moved into the new house anyway and it all worked out fine. But I have to admit, Bob and our real estate agent Leslie and I looked like Curly, Moe, and Larry for a while there.

The warrior is infinitely more tenacious, craftier, more cunning, and more determined than our tyrants, easily diffusing the tyrant's attacks and reminding me that all I need to do is take it in, accept the gifts of the Universe.

What are we willing to let in? Will and intent being qualities of the warrior, they can be used either to manifest or filter, creating and manifesting what we want or need, or convincing us they're beyond our reach. What do we deserve? What do we have the right to ask for? What do we have the responsibility to ask for?

And most important, what happens when we get it? Your tyrants can jump on any of these questions and turn them against you, causing you to shut down to all the possibilities and opportunities to receive virtually anything you want.

It's like having a computer; without knowing how to start the program you don't have access to the computer. With the right code or command, you open up a whole universe of possibilities. How much time do we spend staring at a blank screen, convinced we'll never figure out the right code?

It's like a koan: once you get it, you've gotten it all forever. How much time do we spend trying to figure it out? In life the code that opens the doors to all the Universe has to offer is contained in three words: LET-IT-IN.

I saw an old man the other day, a Clint Eastwood stereotype. He was hard as nails, unemotional, tough, and invulnerable. Clint only plays the part, then he gets to go home and be human. This old man had killed off all the other parts of himself to adopt a caricature. And I thought, how much did he have to leave out? How much effort had he put into keeping out the world's limitless gifts?

When we are in alignment with Grandmother Earth, we let harmony in. When we are out of alignment with Grandmother Earth, we let chaos in. Like any good warrior She will do whatever it takes to establish balance.

Do you remember the fish tank analogy? We are sitting in the midst of all the love, all the abundance, all the peace, all the joy, all the time, all the bliss, all the intelligence, all the beauty there is. And we won't let it in, because we don't think we deserve it. We'd rather believe our tyrants than the truth.

How can we change it? We invoke our warrior to stand up to the tyrants that say we are not good enough, smart enough, loving enough, honest enough, or strong enough. And then we fearlessly examine the places in ourselves where we have given up our love, our honor, our will, our time, our power, and we take it back by letting it in. We align our will with Universal Will, and we let in harmony. We align our mind with Divine Mind, and we let in wisdom. We align our hearts with Universal Love, and we let in bliss. God is willing to give it to us anyway. But having also given us free will, we can choose not to have it.

So go inside and ask. Find your still point. With your breath, find your center, between your pubic bone and your navel. Go into soft focus and continue to breathe yourself into that place until you feel a sense of that space relaxing and opening up. Ask, "What is your will for me?" Listen for the answer. And let it in. Answers will come in many forms: an inner voice, a daydream, feeling drawn to a person, activity, or a place, a new opportunity opening up to you, or even something as mundane as feeling you should call a friend. The answers often come in unexpected ways. There is a certain quiet excitement about these messages that is unmistakable once we've learned to recognize them. It may take a few times and a little practice before you are attuned to these messages again. That's normal. Remember, a lot of conditioning has gone into teaching us to listen to the voices outside and ignore the messages from inside. But they are always there, and with a little patience you will be able to recognize and trust them again.

Contrary to popular religious myth, God doesn't care anything about deserving. God's love isn't conditional. He doesn't hold back love until we have proved that we are worthy. Even the worst mass murderer has God's love, although I doubt they can let it in. And that is the fall from grace—the worst punishment of all and one we inflict on ourselves.

I remember listening to an interview with Jeffrey Dahmer's father, who said that although he believed his son did commit one of the most heinous mass murders of all times, he still felt a great deal of love for him. Visiting his son nearly every day in his jail cell, the father said he would support his son in every way he could. Even so, there were times when the father literally dropped to his knees and wept for the victims and their families. It sickened and horrified him that any human being could commit such acts. When the father was asked if he thought his son could take in the love he had for him, the older Dahmer replied, "Perhaps only a little bit, from time to time." The lesson in this is that no matter what our situation in life, we only have to let in what we need and we will have it.

The times that I forget to ask, when I buy into my tyrant's code that I have to do it all by myself, I run out of time; I run out of money; I run out of energy; I run out of joy; I run on my finite human resources; I run out of gas; I run into a wall. Then I hear the voice of my warrior telling me that I am having an ego attack. And she reminds me to let it go. And I remember that we are not in this alone. Let it in.

The warrior reminds us that our tyrants are our own creations. We project them out into the world so that we may face them, own them, and integrate them. When we learn that this is how it works, our tyrants can no longer stand between us and God. The warrior knows that it is through our ability to receive God's gifts that we are able to develop our own gifts to the Universe completing the Divine cycle of giving and receiving that fulfills our lives.

*T*RY THIS

As you go through your day notice the times you refuse to accept a gift, no matter how small, from someone or something. It may be as simple as someone offering to share something of theirs, or the clerk at the grocery store giving you the penny to simplify your change, or the book you want to buy but don't let yourself have, or your dog wanting to play when you think you don't have time. Instead of refusing, accept what's offered by others. Notice how you feel when you do. Let yourself have one thing each day that you normally would have passed up because you thought you couldn't afford the time, energy, or money, or you thought there might be strings attached. Notice how you feel when you do accept these gifts. Identify as the voice of your tyrants any unwillingness on your part to accept these gifts. Thank your tyrants for their messages, acknowledging that perhaps they had served you in the past. Then go forward and accept the gifts, receiving them with the same love with which God offers them.

CHAPTER SIXTEEN

Trust—
Letting It Go

*M*ORE OFTEN THAN NOT, life itself, even without the
aid of a teacher, provides us with the greatest
lessons. An example of this is an incident that occurred when
Bob and I were vacationing in the Florida Keys several years
ago. As is often the case, the Universe delivered a lesson to
me in receiving in the form of a tiny creature who would find
her way into our lives. Let me share this story with you.

One of the amazing things about the place where we
stayed in the Keys is that the sun rose in the Atlantic right in
front of our cottage, and set across the street in the Florida
Bay. One evening we were standing in a field watching the
sun go down when a little white cat came running out of the
bushes. She started winding herself around our ankles, standing on her hind legs, and talking to us. She looked about three
months old, thin as a rail. She was very sweet, smart, playful,
gentle, and extremely affectionate. We had been told there
were a lot of wild cats around, and we knew she must be one
of them. I felt an immediate connection to her and I wanted
to take her home. However, Bob and I have a contract about

this; we have to agree on any animal we bring home. Otherwise we would be overrun. You see, I can't pass up any stray animal. Ask any of our friends; most of them have an animal I've found for them. At the peak of my animal rescuing career I had five horses, two llamas, three dogs, three cats, and two birds. Right now we have only one per species, except Mr. and Mrs. Fish. But I wanted this little white cat. So Bob and I had a big fight about it. As a sort of compromise he went and bought her some food, but we left her there.

Reflecting on the incident later that night, I realized what she symbolized for me was myself, when I was little and playful and affectionate. Whenever I tried to throw my paws around someone, they shook me off and walked away, just as we were doing with this little creature. It made me think of all the little ones being born into this world, far too many of them being walked away from, in one way or another. And I felt the old heartache.

Who will take care of the cat? Who will take care of the children? My fear says, no one if I don't. It was about letting go. And it was about trust. Either there is a Divine plan or not. Either God exists, and there is no place where God is not, or God does not exist. If there is a Divine plan I don't need to force my plan on the world. I can let it go, turn it over, surrender it all.

The next evening we went back to search for the white cat. It was raining and we were both dressed for dinner. Bob had already gone back to try and find her several times that day. Though we both wanted to honor our contract about bringing animals into our lives, his love for me had apparently overridden his better judgment. I was willing to let the cat go in order to honor my agreement with Bob, even though my heart hurt; Bob was willing to take her in, even though he realized it was going to be both a big hassle and a big expense to get her home. We walked out into the field where we first saw her, calling her and shaking a box of kibble. She called back to us. By the time we got her into the car, we were both soaked, our clothes were trashed, and dinner out was history.

The white cat was scared but never unsheathed her claws. She knew she was safe.

I don't know the end to this story, except that my heartache is gone. I know I don't own her, she doesn't have to live with me. I also know that because I let her go, here she is, and harmony is restored. I thank this little white cat for being a teacher for me. I'm grateful for our willingness to see how when we both were able to give up what we thought we wanted, we got what we needed which was even more than we wanted.

One of the things that strikes me about the cat is how trusting she is of us, especially coming from where she's been, which was basically a junkyard next to a highway, scraping out her own meager survival. And I can see that, if we fail her (which we won't), she knows that she can trust herself. Beyond that, she instinctually knows that she can trust the same Higher Power that sent us to her.

This cat became a koan for me, and no matter what happens, she delivered her message.

When you find something in your path you have several choices: You can step on it, step over it, step around it, or step up to it. Any of those choices has consequences.

Once home, the little white cat, who we named Mouse, appropriated Mocha's favorite chair in my office. She slowly integrated herself into our household. Our vet told me she wasn't three months, but nine months old, stunted from malnutrition. She will always look like a kitten. It was interesting at first, watching her with the other animals. She was very brave and very respectful. She would get just close enough to either Shilo or Mocha to ensure escape if necessary, not crowding their space, just sitting and hanging out, and watching them, letting them get used to her presence. She was afraid of both of them, but not timid. Mocha is four times her size and she isn't even as big as Shilo's head. She just kept holding her ground, a little warrior cat. We could all take a lesson from her in courage and respect and perseverance and trust.

Mocha, is the size of a small panther. He is (you'd never know it unless you were willing to risk rolling him over on his belly) a fixed male. He terrorizes the neighborhood cats. He goes into their houses and eats their food, and then brings their toys home. Little Mouse, a flyweight, is the model of passive resistance. She simply sits in Mocha's presence, just outside of striking range. She called his bluff. She held her ground, but offered nothing to come up against. There was no place to receive the arrow. She was simply there, and intended to stay there. Interesting strategy. When he simply couldn't stand it and hissed at her and took a swipe, she returned in kind, even though she is one-quarter his size. What she wanted was worth fighting for and getting her little butt kicked for, maybe even dying for. She gave no ground. Her heart was totally in it. She had everything to gain and nothing to lose. Mocha stalked away, his ego not quite intact. But that's not what Mouse brought to the encounter, so she lost nothing, and was willing to lose everything. Her heart was bigger than Mocha's ego.

Somewhere inside the little cat was a truth she trusted unconditionally, enough even to risk her life for. I couldn't help but ask, what would that truth be for me, or you, my readers? Where are the truths we trust so much we are willing to risk everything for them? Until we can each answer that, we don't know what Mouse knows.

Trust and letting go are big issues for all of us, particularly today when many of the patterns we've been following, the way we've been living our lives, have led us to a global crisis. We have begun to question everything. Spending time in Florida, finding Mouse the Cat, watching the sun rise and set over the water, filled me with new commitment to being a global warrior.

The Florida Keys are a beautiful chain of islands, a nat- ural hammock of mangrove and coral reefs. But civilization has driven a stake into its heart. McDonald's and Days Inns abound. Our country has become one, huge strip mall, except in the areas where there is enough money to keep them—and probably me and you—out. My Aunt Mary was talking about the good old days when we were visiting her and Uncle George in Naples. They got to see all the beautiful places, before Taco Bell and industrial waste moved in. Bob asked her what she felt the main difference was between then and now. She said, "Well, we had to work a lot harder. We didn't have all of the conveniences. You couldn't go to the grocery store and buy a can of tomatoes, you had to can them. But, we could still go to Rio, and swim, before the water got too polluted. And Naples was still a charming little beach town instead of a booming metropolis." She talked about the world as she and Uncle George experienced it thirty and forty years ago. It made me very sad to know that I would never be able to see it that way.

A while back, *Time* magazine ran an article talking about the countries of Suriname and Guyana selling their rain forests to Asian consortiums. They say they will probably be clear-cut, turning a paradise into a wasteland. The Asian countries doing the bidding once had some of the largest tropical rain forests on the planet but they wasted them, not bothering to consider what kind of impact this would have on the global community.

Further, there are strains of lethal viruses, called *filoviruses*, coming out of the rain forests, which kill horribly and rapidly, and for which we have no cure. I hope you can appreciate the irony of this. Did you think She was just going to sit there and take it? These viruses are integral to the regional ecosystem which is being destroyed. Out of context with that ecosystem, placed in another, they become lethal, reminding us once again of how important it is to acknowledge and respect all those systems and life-forms other than our own.

When we were in the Florida Keys Bob learned that the jet skis, buzzing around the water like mosquitoes, are ruining many forms of sea life. But the lure of money to be made with them from tourists is too tempting for the locals to outlaw them. He also learned that the sugarcane industry has diverted all the freshwater out of the Bay. The freshwater keeps the algae growth down; without it, the algae has taken over and the Bay is out of balance, becoming quite overgrown with the stuff.

We can't go out in the sun. We can't drink the water. Be sure to scrub or peel the vegetables. Forget Caesar's salad; you've got to cook the egg or risk salmonella poisoning. We can't breathe the air. That's all four elements: Earth, Air, Fire, Water. At least we're thorough. We've poisoned our planet and our poisons are coming right back to us.

If we continue on this course, pretty soon we won't have air to breath or water to drink. How does it make you feel that some country on the opposite side of the globe is making decisions that will ultimately affect your life without checking with you first? Now, here's the big question. What can you and I do about it?

It's clear that we've got to change but we're surrounded by tyrants, both within and without, telling us it's too late to turn back. Our tyrants say given the lifestyle we've created, we can't change. But, because of our current crisis, we need to muster all the skills of the warrior. In this case, it has to do with letting go. In the martial arts, if something isn't working, we change the angle, the tactic, the strike, the target, the timing, whatever it takes; we let go of what isn't working and find another way to deliver the technique. If we don't, we find our ass on the mat. Now here's the trick. Sometimes before we can let in something that will work, we have to let go of whatever isn't working. There is a point where we are suspended in *not knowing*. We step off the edge and trust that underneath are the everlasting arms. We have to let go of the rope. That moment is critical to our enlightenment, and our survival. Because, the bottom line is if we don't trust God we can't trust anything, and we will continue along our path of destruction. Letting go of our habits, even though they are destructive and painful, is difficult, because at least they're familiar. We are being asked to step off the edge, step into the unknown, and trust our warrior to guide us. Like the little white cat, the warrior knows there is always something on the other side, that

Source won't leave us without an alternative, and in fact, an alternative that is an improvement over what we've been doing. However, letting go at this level can feel like death, and in fact it is a form of death. Death to an era, death to a system that is no longer working; death to the ego. What the Higher Self knows that the ego doesn't know is that only the ego dies. Who we really are is infinite and eternal. Trust makes it possible for us to let go. Trust assures us that we cannot fail, or fall too far before we are caught by the everlasting arms.

Can we let go of what we've got, what we've been doing, because it isn't working? Can we trust ourselves to step into the unknown, and find something that will work? What would we do if we didn't have all of our stuff? What would we do if we didn't have our addictions? What would we do if we didn't have things to do, places to go, people to see? What would we feel if we let go of our blame? What would we say if we let go of our kvetching? What would we have if we let go of our greed? What would we be if we let go of our fear?

LETTING IT GO

What in your life are you unwilling to let go of? Whatever it is, it owns you.

If we are not yet ready to surrender everything, and Lord knows I'm not, we can at least replace one attachment for another, less destructive one. We can start right now by asking ourselves, what can we do instead?

I'm not ready to give up my car, but at least I make sure the one I have doesn't pollute and is big enough to transport others who are ready to give up theirs. If you're not ready to give up the pretensions of fancy clothes, at least be sure somebody didn't have to sacrifice their skin so that you could wear it.

If you're not ready to let go of your money, be sure that the way you're making it isn't damaging the earth or taking away from something or somebody else.

If you're not ready to give up food, be sure what you're eating is a gift and not a theft, that it will nurture and not poison you, and that its production isn't harming the earth.

If we all take just one, small step toward the truth, toward evolution, toward each other, toward honoring Grandmother Earth, we can change our world.

It all comes down to trust. Look at your three primary energy centers: head, heart, and moving center. Do you trust yourself? This involves the moving center. If you don't, why not? What do you have to change to be able to trust yourself? Do you trust yourself to take care of yourself physically? Can you be responsible for your own survival? Can you protect yourself or others from violence? Can you handle yourself in a dangerous situation? If not, do something about it. A warrior knows that without this as your base, the other centers have nothing to build upon.

Do you trust others? This comes from the heart center. What do *you* have to change? (Not what do *they* have to change.) It is your warrior that takes risks, and most of us have already learned there is great risk in opening our hearts. In doing so there are no guarantees that our love will be reciprocated. But we still need to trust. We can't afford to wait and see if our world will love us first; we have to love our world, even if we are afraid. The heart center is the seat of our conscience, so when we allow ourselves to love, we also allow ourselves to see where we have harmed others, and to experience their pain. Someone once said to me, trusting others is about being able to say, "I trust you to be who you are, and I see you. Not for what I want you to be, but for who you really are." So it comes back to trusting ourselves. Under the glaring light of that reality, with all our imperfections spotlighted, that's where we learn what trust is really about.

Do you trust the Universe? If not, what do you need to change? I believe this comes down to, can you be trusted? I used to think this meant I could never make mistakes; I came to learn that it just meant I had to own them, and clean them up when I made them.

While trust is essential, change only occurs by taking action. One of the elements of trust is knowing that someone will *follow through*. And this action begins by asking, and answering, questions such as:

- What will it take?
- What will we have to give up?
- What will we get?
- And most important, what if we don't change and continue on our present course of action?

What will *it take* to save our forests? The appropriate actions we must risk will obviously require sacrifices. Here are some suggestions for where we might begin:

Support the use of products that are native to forests and are renewable resources. Products such as nuts and certain herbs actually encourage the preservation of the forests, providing income for the local economy and encouraging governments to protect what nature provides rather than going along with the false promises of those who would exploit the forests and the indigenous people.

Don't use any products taken from the rain forests that deplete them; boycott the places that sell them; support the organizations that are trying to save them; and go after the organizations that are trying to destroy them.

We'll have to *give up* redwood decks, mahogany furniture, and whatever else comes from endangered forests. We'll have to give up a certain amount of convenience, a certain amount of time while we figure out what we can use instead. For instance, many furniture companies as well as builders are using pine, which grows quickly and lends itself to "tree farming." We'll have to give up being nice to the people who contribute to the destruction of the forests. We'll have to give up our silence. We'll have to give up our apathy.

Though we might sacrifice some convenience, we'll be getting back something much more valuable. We'll *get* to have our self-respect back. We'll *get* to have our integrity back.

We'll get to be worthy of trust. We'll get to be back in alignment. We'll get to have our world back.

Or, eventually, maybe in the not too distant future, we won't have a world at all. I don't have anyplace else to go, do you?

Take one thing that you do today and follow it out to its natural conclusion. See how it impacts your world. Watch and pay attention. See what comes into your life when you clear some space by eliminating the things you have and the things you do that don't support the planet.

*T*RY THIS

1. Look at the areas of your life where you know you are doing something harmful to others or to the planet. Write them down, be very clear and ruthlessly honest.

2. Ask yourself how it would affect your life if you were willing to let these harmful practices go, sacrifice them to a Higher Power. Examine how it would inconvenience you on a purely practical level, and measure that inconvenience against the harm it is doing, and the way it makes you feel about yourself.

3. Ask yourself whether you can trust that Higher Power to replace the harmful object or situation if you risk letting it go, even before you know what it would be replaced with. What do you *need* to be able to take that risk, to let go and change? This is where the warrior pushes the edge, and where you have to trust your warrior as you step into the unknown.

4. As you explore these questions use the tools you have been given in earlier chapters to ground yourself in your moving center, and to identify the voice of the ego and the voice of your Higher Self.

$\mathcal{A}$UTHORITY AND LETTING GO

Even on the subject of letting go, I find my animal friends to be some of my best teachers. Here they remind me not to divide the world between friends and enemies. Letting go includes letting go of our judgments, even while being discriminating about what we allow in our lives. For instance, even though Mocha is a tyrant, we still love him, not in spite of or even because of, but simply because we love him. We know that he reflects to us, as Mouse does, a part of ourselves. We thank him for being a teacher. But, if necessary, in order to maintain fairness and balance, we are willing to step in. We won't let him hurt Mouse. And there is an Authority, who will step in if it gets too far out of balance, if we can't find our own authority. If that happens, we will, for a time, give up a lot of choices, since we proved we couldn't be trusted with them. Like taking a car away from a teenager who crashes it, or who doesn't get home on time. I hope it doesn't come to that. It's still up to us. But the window is closing. Let's get it right this time.

CHAPTER SEVENTEEN

The Warrior's Frontier

WHEN JESUS WAS ON THE MOUNTAINTOP, and Satan was tempting him, all Jesus had to do was deny his spirituality and he could have had all that the material world offered. What if he had said yes? What would he have become? The answer might be that he would have become what we have become.

Jesus knew something that made it possible for him to refuse the devil's deal. The warrior—and I believe Jesus was a great warrior—knows what that is; like Jesus, the warrior knows:

> You can run out of gas,
> You can run out of money,
> You can run out of time.
> But you can't run out of God.

So, like Christ, the warrior knows that all of the things Satan tempts us with, in exchange for our denying our God Self, are already ours. Jesus knew that he was God, and God is All That Is. Only there is a different price tag on God's gifts. While God's gifts are freely given, we can't own them; we can

161

only enjoy them. We also learn that these gifts can't own us. The price for all this is surrender. We have to absolutely put our trust in the Absolute.

We have conquered all the frontiers, except one. That is ourselves and our need to conquer instead of living side by side with all of the other ideas that God has created. There is a metaphysical principle that says, it's never too late to change the material picture. That picture is projected by our consciousness, and our consciousness is what we need to change. As warriors, this is our new frontier. How we hold the world in ourselves will change how we hold ourselves in the world. We have lost our sense of joy, our sense of humor, our sense of wonder, and have traded them for temporal things. We have traded our innocence for technology, we've traded our families for our fantasies, we've traded freedom for license and we're beginning to wake up to the fact that it was a bad deal. So what's left is how we're going to deal with what we've done. Ask yourself, "What can I do to make a difference?" And if you're not doing it, ask yourself, "What stops me?" And find a way to do it anyway. If you choose to take the warrior's path, you will find that you have all the resources you need to make the changes you want to make in your life, to take your power back, and prosper in the times to come.

Integrity has come to mean consistency within a given system. That means we can complete the destruction of this planet and still be in our integrity. But that kind of integrity is pure ego. There is a point where we must turn to the integrity of the power greater than ourselves: call it Cosmic Law. Do we really want to put ego above this Higher Self? We have to ask ourselves some difficult questions, and then be prepared to deal with the answers.

What do we have to do to survive as a species? We have to give up our belief in separation; separation from Source; separation from each other; separation from the other species that inhabit this planet; separation from our dark side. We have to stop hiding the parts of ourselves we don't love and embrace them. We have to stop acting as if what I do over here doesn't impact you over there; we have to stop acting as if we don't care; we have to stop acting as if we don't know.

We have to learn to risk more, love more, give more. We have to put our asses on the line, stand up to our tyrants even if we die, because if we don't, we will. We have to ask ourselves what is this costing me? What is this costing you? The bill has come due. We are looking at some hard choices, and how we choose will determine if we survive as a species. Your warrior is here to support you to stand in your truth and make the right choices.

Your warrior gives you the courage to find your right place in the Universe. Each of us has an internal understanding of what path best serves us; when we allow ourselves to align with that path we usually find that it serves the collective as well. One of the greatest qualities of a warrior is service to a cause bigger than him or herself. More than at any other time in our history, this planet needs all our gifts.

Your warrior's heart will help you find your right family in the Universe. I encourage each of you to find the places in your life, the people in your life, where you feel community and a sense of purpose, and develop them as your base. Find each other. Strategize together. Create a safe place to return to, people you can trust as your home base. This is where you come for support, for love, and for advice. This is where you come to laugh, or cry, to let it out, to let it down. This is where you offer your gifts, and where they are received. This is where you let yourself care and be cared for. This is the place and these are the people you would give your life for, and give your life to. Listen to the nagging feeling in the back of your consciousness that tells you something is missing in your life, and go after it. Be willing to stretch yourself and give more. Bring yourself forward and offer your gifts, and be willing to receive the gifts of others. You have the right to ask for as much as you can give, and the responsibility to accept nothing less. A warrior refuses mediocrity, refuses the half-truths, refuses to accept anything other than her or his own brilliance. There is an axiom I use when I choose the word "family." It is, who would I want at my back if the worst should go down? The people to whom I have made that commitment know I would lay my life down for them, and I am willing to accept nothing less from them; it would diminish them if I expected less from them. Ask yourself that question. Who would I want at my back? Find those people and include them in your life. Become that kind of person. This is such an important part of what warrior work is all about.

No one can do the work for you. A good teacher is just someone who's made it across the mine field, who stands on the other side, and tells you where the mines are so that you can make it across in one piece. At this time on the planet, our teachers are trying to keep us from blowing ourselves up.

To whatever degree we've owned our warrior will determine how we survive the coming changes. And they are coming! We've already crossed a line. There are species that are extinct, and we will never see them again. There are forests we have cut down and we will never be able to walk through them again. There are rivers so polluted we will never swim in them again. Balance is about to be restored, and that is often preceded by chaos. Fasten your seat belts, we're about to go for a ride.

As the events get more mesmerizing, keep coming back to your center, to who you are in this moment, to the place where your warrior lives. And live your life, make your choices from the place of your warrior. The commitment to do so will determine the quality of your life, the quality of your relationships, and the quality of your world now and in the future.

An old samurai saying goes, "A Warrior first conquers himself." The rest is easy.

I don't mean to imply that you're done once you've owned your warrior. The work continues, the lessons become subtler, but as you become more skilled in your ability to learn them, you begin to enjoy the game. That point is detachment. That point is surrender. That point is being willing to put everything you have, everything you think you know, everything you are, on the line. Because whatever you think you have to lose, owns you. You can't serve two masters, not if you want freedom. This is the secret that Christ and every great warrior has known.

The Irish poet and playwright, William Butler Yeats, once said that in developing our lives to the higher levels we can "make our minds so like still water" that people will gather around us and perhaps see their own image in us, and for the moment live with "a clearer, perhaps fiercer life because of our quiet."

What's really going on is an opportunity to take our lives up to the next level. It may look like it's breaking down, but we're really breaking through. There will be some tough challenges, and your warrior is equal to them. You will even find exhilaration in meeting the task. It will be straightening by fire, but your warrior will guide you safely through. You are about to realize how powerful you really are.

Having accomplished the task at hand, resolved conflicts both internal and external, what will the warrior do? The warrior becomes the magician

Like a Phoenix from the embers
Ashes to ashes
Burning, burning
Some by fire
Some by water
Until we remember returning.

Some by the arts of the necromancer
Some by the sword
Some in the trance of the Sufi dancer
Some by the word.

Prodigal daughter
Walks the Warrior's path
Some by water
Some by tempting God to laugh.

Woman's body
Warrior's soul
Dance the ancient rite
Free the dragons of desire
Into the Light
Some by fire.

Author Biography

Dawn Callan has dedicated her life to the skills of living, philosophy, spirituality and physical training. Not only have these disciplines shaped her life's journey, they have provided her a deeply satisfying life's work, earning her the respect of the martial arts and metaphysical communities.

Though the holder of 6th degree Black Belts in Chinese Kenpo and Kobra Kaj Karate, with 26 years of training in Choai Lai Fut Kung Fu, Wing Chun Kung Fu, and Hop Gar Kun Fu, she says that the martial arts have taught her more about how to live than how to fight.

She served for several years as a body guard for celebrities and other high profile clients and is certified for teaching Police control and restraint techniques.

As the founder and facilitator of Awakening the Warrior Within Workshops, she has trained over 3,000 students.

Her teaching and training is valued by corporations, universities, and police departments throughout the U.S.

She has appeared on national television, radio shows, and in feature articles in the national print media.

Dawn is a mother, gardener, and vegetarian gourmet cook.

Tenacity Press

Our desire is to create books for readers much like ourselves, interested in creativity, personal growth, and spiritual development. We choose our books carefully, working only with authors with whom we feel a common bond.

Our authors are available to speak about their books or to facilitate workshops.

If you wish any further information, either about our authors or our other titles, please call the following toll-free number:

1-800-738-6721